PREPOSITIONS

put off: postpone	We cannot put off the meeting again.
reel off: recite a long list	She reeled off a long list of names.
rope in: persuade to help	We roped in everyone we could to help with the work.
rub out: erase	Be sure to rub out all the pencil marks.
scale down: reduce	Because of lack of funds, we had to scale down our plans.
sell off: dispose of by selling	We sold off all the books and furniture.
set back: delay	This could set back the project by several years.
single out: [illegible]	[illegible] singled out for special mention.
size up: assess	I quickly sized up the situation.
sort out: organise	It will take some time to sort out this mess.
stammer out: [illegible]	[illegible] stammered out [illegible]
sum up: summarise	He summed up the discussion in a few well-chosen words.
summon up: gather	[illegible] to summon up [illegible]
take in: absorb	[illegible] to take in the new information.
take out: invite to a restaurant	May I take you out for supper?
take over: assume control	They will take over at the beginning of June.
talk over: discuss	Let us talk it over before we decide.
tear up: destroy by tearing	She tore up the letter.
think over: consider	I need some time to think it over.
think up: invent	What will they think up next?

PREPOSITIONS

Josna Sebastian

Commonwealth

Prepositions

First Published : 2009

ISBN 978-81-311-0241-1

Published by :
COMMONWEALTH PUBLISHERS PVT. LTD.
4831/24, Prahlad Street,
Ansari Road, Darya Ganj,
New Delhi - 110002
Ph. : 23272541, 23257835
Fax : 91- 011- 23257835
e-mail : campusbooks@hotmail.com

Laser Typesetting by :
Dimple Typesetter
Delhi

Printed at :
Roshan Offset Printers
Delhi

Preface

A preposition links nouns, pronouns and phrases to other words in a sentence. The word or phrase that the preposition introduces is called the object of the preposition. A preposition usually indicates the temporal, spatial or logical relationship of its object to the rest of the sentence.

A preposition is a part of speech that introduces a prepositional phrase. A prepositional phrase is made up of the preposition, its object and any associated adjectives or adverbs. A prepositional phrase can function as a noun, an adjective, or an adverb. In English, the most used prepositions are "of", "to", "in", "for", and "on". Simply put, a preposition indicates a relation between things mentioned in a sentence.

Requirement of appropriate preposition for appropriate occasion is inevitable. Only with a good knowledge of prepositions one can express the thoughts and feelings meticulously. This book provides all essential information about prepositions and their usage. It is hoped that it would help young scholars to develop in-depth knowledge of prepositions commonly used in English.

Josna Sebastian

Contents

	Preface	*v*
1.	Introduction to Prepositions	1
2.	Preposition and Postposition	42
3.	List of English Prepositions	62
4.	Place Prepositions	66
5.	Preposition of Time : at, in, all	70
6.	Phrasal Verbs Followed by Preposition	78
7.	Verbs that Take Prepositions	112
8.	Use of "To" and "Through"	117
9.	Grammatical Analysis of Prepositions	147
10.	Detection of Prepositional Errors	166
	Bibliography.	*179*

1

Introduction to Prepositions

A word such as a noun, pronoun or gerund following a preposition is said to be the object of the preposition. A personal pronoun following a preposition must be in the objective case. A phrase beginning with a preposition can be referred to as a prepositional phrase. The prepositional phrases in the following examples are underlined.

e.g. He owns the house on the corner.

— We are waiting for her.

— She has read many books about flying.

In the first example, the noun corner is the object of the preposition on. In the second example, the personal pronoun her is the object of the preposition for. It can be seen that the personal pronoun her is in the objective case. In the third example, the gerund flying is the object of the preposition about.

A preposition serves to connect its object with the rest of a sentence. In doing so, a preposition indicates the relationship of the idea expressed in the prepositional phrase to the ideas expressed In the rest of the sentence. For instance in the sentence *He owns the house on the corner,* the preposition on indicates that the words *the corner* express the location of the house referred to in the rest of the sentence. Similarly, in the sentence *We are waiting for her,* the preposition *for* indicates that the word *her* expresses the reason for the action of waiting referred to in the rest of the sentence.

Although there are fewer than one hundred English prepositions, although prepositions do not take endings, and although the structure of most prepositional phrases is simple, the use of English prepositions is very complex. The reasons for this are that most prepositions have more than one meaning, many prepositions can also be used as adverbs, prepositions are used in hundreds of idioms, many adjectives, nouns, and verbs must usually be followed by certain prepositions, and there are hundreds of phrasal verbs formed from combinations of verbs with adverbs and prepositions.

It should also be noted that the use of prepositions varies somewhat among the different dialects of English. For instance, as illustrated in the following example, there are some differences between British and North American English in the use of prepositions.

e.g. British Usage: There is a fence about the garden.

— American Usage: There is a fence around the garden.

MEANINGS OF PREPOSITIONS

The table below gives the most usual meanings of

English prepositions. Each meaning is illustrated by an example.

About

1. *On the subject of*: This is a story about elephants.
2. *Approximately*: He is about ten years old.

Above

1. *Higher than; over*: The plane flew above the clouds.
2. *Earlier on a page*: There is a heading above each diagram.

Across

1. *From one side to the other*: We walked across the field.
2. *On the other side of*: There is a store across the street.

After

1. *Later in time*: after ten o'clock; after lunch
2. *Later in a series*: Q comes after P in the alphabet.
3. *In pursuit of*: The dog ran after the cat.

Against

1. *In opposition to*: Theft is against the law.
2. *Touching; supported by*: I leaned my bicycle against the wall.

Along

1. *Following the length of*: We walked along the road.

Among

1. *Within a group*: The money was shared among three people.

Around

1. *Circling something*: We walked around the block.
2. *Surrounding*: There is a fence around the garden.
3. *In different parts of*: I looked around the house for the keys.
4. *In the other direction:* We turned around and went back home.
5. *Approximately*: He is around six feet tall.

At

1. *A specific location*: at 23 Chestnut Street; at the park
2. *A point in time*: at 5 o'clock; at Christmas
3. *A condition*: at peace; at war; at rest
4. *An activity*: at work; at school; at play
5. *Towards*: Look at someone; wave at someone

When referring to a specific location or to a point in time, at is usually used. When referring to a certain street or a certain day, on is usually used. When referring to a location as an area, or when referring to a unit of time longer than a day, in is usually used.

e.g. at Christmas; on Christmas day; in the Christmas

holidays

Before

1. *Earlier in time*: before two o'clock; before Christmas
2. *Earlier in a series*: S comes before T in the alphabet.

Behind

1. *At the back of*: The little girl hid behind her mother.
2. *Late*: I am behind in my work.
3. *Cause; origin*: Who was behind that idea?

Below

1. *Lower than; under*: below freezing; below sea level
2. *Later on a page*: Footnotes are provided below the text.

Beneath

1. *Lower than; below*: beneath the earth

Beside

1. *Next to; at the side of*: I sit beside her in class.

Besides

1. *Also; as well as*: We study other languages besides English.

The differing meanings of beside and besides. Beside is usually used with reference to a physical location.

Between

1. *An intermediate location*: Toronto lies between Montreal and Vancouver.
2. *An intermediate time*: between Christmas and New Year's Day
3. *Intermediate in a series*: B comes between A and C in the alphabet.
4. *An intermediate amount*: between five and ten people
5. *Within a group of two*: The money was shared between two people.

Beyond

1. *Farther than*: The mountains lie beyond the horizon.
2. *Further than; exceeding*: That was beyond my expectations.

But

1. *Except*: I have read all but the last chapter.

But is used more often as a conjunction than as a preposition.

By

1. *Near*: a house by the sea
2. *Past*: He waved as he drove by the house.
3. *Not later than*: Try to finish the work by next week.
4. *In units of*: cheaper by the dozen; sold by weight

5. *Through the means of*: travel by plane; written by him

By is often used in combination with verbs in the Passive Voice.

Concerning

1. *Connected with; about*: He studies everything concerning trees.

Despite

1. *In spite of*: We walked downtown despite the rain.

Down

1. *To a lower position*: The ball rolled down the hill.
2. *Further along*: He lives down the street.

During

1. *Throughout a period*: She works during the day.
2. *Sometime within a period*: An accident occurred during the night.

Except

1. *Not including*: I have visited everyone except him.

For

1. *Duration of time*: We walked for two hours.
2. *Distance*: I walked for five kilometers.
3. *Purpose*: I bought this jacket for you.

4. *In the direction of*: She left for New York.
5. *In favor of*: We are for the proposal.
6. *Considering*: The boy is clever for his age.

From

1. *Place of origin*: We left from Boston; he comes from Mexico
2. *Start of a period of time*: from now on; from yesterday until today
3. *Start of a range*: From 20 to 30 people were present.
4. *Cause*: He suffers from nervousness.
5. *Source*: I first heard the story from you.

In

1. *Place thought of as an area*: in London; in Europe
2. *Within a location*: in the room; in the building
3. *Large units of time*: That happened in March, in 1992.
4. *Within a certain time*: I will return in an hour.
5. *By means of*: write in pencil; speak in English
6. *Condition*: in doubt; in a hurry; in secret
7. *A member of*: He is in the orchestra; in the navy
8. *Wearing*: the boy in the blue shirt
9. *With reference to*: lacking in ideas; rich in oil

Inside

1. *Within*: They are inside the house.

Into

1. *To the inside of*: We stepped into the room.
2. *Change of condition*: The boy changed into a man.

Like

1. *Resembling*: That looks like him.
2. *Appearing possible*: It looks like rain.
3. *Be in a suitable mood for*: I feel like going swimming.

Minus

1. *Less*: Three minus two equals one.

Near

1. *Close to*: near the school; near the ocean

Of

1. *Location*: east of here; the middle of the road
2. *Possession*: a friend of mine; the sound of music
3. *Part of a group*: one of us; a member of the team
4. *Measurement*: a cup of milk; two meters of snow

Off

1. *Not on; away from*: Please keep off the grass.
2. *At some distance from*: There are islands off the coast.

On

1. *Touching the surface of*: on the table; on the wall

2. *A certain day*: That happened on Sunday, on the 6th of June.
3. *A certain street*: on South Street
4. *About*: a book on engineering
5. *A state or condition*: on strike; on fire; on holiday
6. *By means of*: live on a pension; shown on television

Onto

1. *To a position on*: The child climbed onto the table.

Opposite

1. *Facing*: The library is opposite the fire station.

Out of

1. *To the outside of*: She went out of the room.
2. *From among*: We won two games out of three.
3. *Motive*: We spoke to them out of politeness.
4. *Material*: The bridge is made out of steel.
5. *Beyond*: out of control; out of danger

Outside

1. *On the outer side of*: outside the house
2. *Beyond the limits of*: outside my experience

Over

1. *Above; higher than*: There are cupboards over the sink.

2. *Covering*: We spread an extra blanket over the bed.
3. *Across*: I jumped over a puddle.
4. *More than*: It cost over ten dollars; it took over an hour
5. *During*: I saw him several times over the past week.
6. *By means of*: We made plans over the telephone.

Past

1. *Up to and beyond*: I walked past the house.
2. *After (in time)*: It was past 2 o'clock; half past two
3. *Beyond*: past belief

Per

1. *For each*: 60 kilometers per hour; price per liter

Plus

1. *With the addition of*: Six plus four equals ten.

Since

1. *From a specific time in the past*: I had been waiting since two o'clock.
2. *From a past time until now*: I have been waiting here since noon.

Because of its meaning, the preposition since is usually used in combination with a perfect tense. It should be noted that the preposition for can also be used with a perfect tense. However, when used with reference to time, for is usually followed by a phrase referring to a period of time; whereas since is usually followed by a phrase referring to a specific time.

e.g. I have known him for six months.

— I have known him since January.

In the first example, for is followed by six months, which refers to a period of time. In the second example, since is followed by January, which refers to a specific time.

Through

1. *Across; from end to end of*: the main road through town
2. *For the whole of a period*: I slept through the night.
3. *By means of*: Skill improves through practice.

Throughout

1. *In every part of*: throughout the world
2. *For the whole of a period*: throughout the winter

Till

Till can be used instead of until. However, at the beginning of a sentence, until is usually used.

To

1. *In the direction of*: Turn to the right.
2. *Destination*: I am going to Rome.
3. *Until*: from Monday to Friday; five minutes to ten

4. *Compared with*: They prefer hockey to soccer.
5. *With indirect object*: Please give it to me.
6. *As part of infinitive*: I like to ski; he wants to help.
7. *In order to*: We went to the store to buy soap.

Toward (or Towards)

1. *In the direction of*: We walked toward the center of town.
2. *Near; just before (time)*: It rained towards evening.

Under

1. *Beneath*: under the desk; under the trees
2. *Less than*: Under 100 people were present.
3. *In circumstances of*: under repair; under way; under discussion

Underneath

1. *Below, under*: underneath the carpet

Until

1. *Up to a certain time*: She will stay until Friday; until 5 p.m.

Upon

On and upon have similar meanings. Upon may be used in certain expressions, as in once upon a time, and following certain verbs, as in to rely upon someone.

Up

1. *To a higher place*: We went up the stairs.
2. *In a higher place*: She lives up the hill.

Up to

1. *As far as*: up to now; I have read up to page 100.
2. *Depending on*: The decision is up to you.
3. *As good as; ready for*: His work is up to standard.

Versus

1. *Against (sports, legal)*: The next game is England versus Australia.

Via

1. *By way of*: He went to Los Angeles via San Francisco.

With

1. *Accompanying*: He came with her; I have my keys with me.
2. *Having; containing*: Here is a book with a map of the island.
3. *By means of; using*: I repaired the shoes with glue.
4. *Manner*: with pleasure; with ease; with difficulty
5. *Because of*: We were paralyzed with fear.

Within

1. *Inside of*: within twenty minutes; within one kilometer

Without

1. *Not having*: Do not leave without your coat; without money

PREPOSITIONS USED IN IDIOMS

Below are examples of idioms consisting of prepositional phrases. The following selection of idioms emphasizes those used in North American English. The meaning of each idiom is indicated after the colon.

At

- *not at all*: not in any way
- *at all times*: always
- *at any rate*: whatever happens
- *keep someone at arm's length*: avoid becoming closely involved with someone
- *at close quarters*: very near
- *at one's disposal*: to be used as one wishes
- *at a distance*: not near
- *at fault*: causing something wrong
- *at first*: at the beginning
- *see at a glance*: see immediately
- *at hand*: near; readily available
- *at last*: finally, after some delay
- *at a loss*: uncertain what to do or say
- *at the mercy of*: without defense against
- *at the moment*: now

- *at once*: immediately
- *at present*: now
- *at rest*: not moving
- *at risk*: threatened by danger or loss
- *at short notice*: with little warning
- *at stake*: to be won or lost
- *at a stretch*: continuously
- *at that rate*: under those circumstances
- *at this point*: at this place; at this moment
- *at the wheel*: in control

Behind

- *behind the scenes*: (of persons) influencing events secretly; (in a theater) behind the stage
- *behind schedule*: not on time

Beside

- *be beside oneself*: lose one's self-control
- *beside the point*: irrelevant

Between

- *read between the lines*: deduce a meaning that
- is not actually expressed

Beyond

- *beyond help*: unable to be helped
- *beyond a joke*: too annoying to be amusing
- *beyond reproach*: perfect; blameless

By

- *by accident*: not deliberately
- *by all means*: by any possible method
- *bit by bit*: gradually
- *by chance*: by accident; without planning
- *by courtesy of*: with the help or permission of
- *win by default*: win because of lack of competition
- *by degrees*: gradually
- *perform by ear*: perform (music) by listening to the sound, without referring to written music
- *by hand*: without the use of machinery
- *by heart*: from memory
- *little by little*: gradually
- *by means of*: by using
- *by mistake*: accidentally
- *by no means*: not at all
- *one by one*: one at a time
- *by oneself*: alone
- *side by side*: beside one another
- *by the way*: incidentally (used to introduce an unrelated topic of conversation)
- *by word of mouth*: orally

For

- *once and for all*: for the last time (e.g. used when giving someone a final warning)

— *for certain*: definitely; without doubt
— *for a change*: for the sake of variety
— *for example*: as an illustration
— *for fun*: for the sake of enjoyment
— *for good*: permanently
— *for good measure*: in addition to the necessary amount
— *for instance*: for example; as an illustration
— *for keeps*: (colloquial) permanently
— *for a living*: as a profession
— *for now*: temporarily
— *run for office*: compete for an elected position
— *for one thing*: because of one reason (out of several)
— *for the sake of*: for the benefit of; for the purpose of
— *for sale*: intended to be sold
— *for sure*: definitely (more colloquial than for certain)
— *food for thought*: something which makes one think
— *play for time*: delay doing something in the hope that the situation will improve
— *for the time being*: until some other arrangement is made
— *ask for trouble*: act in a dangerous or foolish way
— *for a while*: for a period of time

- *word for word*: exactly as said or written

From

- *from afar*: from a distance
- *from all sides*: from all directions
- *from head to foot*: (of a person) completely; all over
- *from scratch*: from the beginning
- *from time to time*: occasionally

In

- *in addition to*: as well as
- *in advance*: before
- *be in agreement with*: have the same opinion as
- *in any case*: whatever happens
- *in brief*: in a few words
- *in bulk*: (of goods) in large amounts; not in packages
- *be in charge of*: have responsibility for
- *in common*: shared by all members of a group
- *in control*: having the power to direct something
- *in the course of*: during
- *in danger*: likely to be harmed
- *in a daze*: unable to think clearly; confused
- *in debt*: owing money
- *in demand*: (of goods or persons) desired by many people
- *in depth*: (investigate something) thoroughly

— *in detail*: (explain something) thoroughly
— *in disgrace*: regarded with disapproval because of having done something wrong
— *in the distance*: far away
— *in doubt*: uncertain
— *in duplicate*: so that there are two identical copies (of a document)
— *in earnest*: seriously; in a determined way
— *in effect*: (of rules) operating
— *in the end*: finally
— *in fact*: in reality; really
— *in fashion*: fashionable; accepted as being the most desirable and up to date
— *in favor of*: supporting (an idea)
— *in flames*: burning, with visible flames
— *in a flash*: very quickly; suddenly
— *in full*: without omitting anything
— *in general*: usually; as a whole
— *hand in hand*: (of persons) holding hands; (of related situations) occurring together
— *in a hurry*: trying to accomplish something quickly
— *in jest*: as a joke
— *in kind*: (payment) in goods rather than in money
— *in itself*: without reference to anything else
— *in league with*: (of persons) joined together with

(usually for a dishonest purpose)

- *be in the limelight*: be the focus of attention; receive great publicity
- *in the long run*: in the end; eventually
- *in the long term*: looking ahead to the distant future
- *leave someone in the lurch*: abandon someone who is in a difficult situation
- *BE IN THE MINORITY*: be in the smaller of two groups
- *in mint condition*: (of manufactured goods) perfect; brand-new
- *in a minute*: soon
- *in a moment*: soon; quickly
- *set something in motion*: start something going
- *nip something in the bud*: put an end to something before it gets properly started
- *in no time*: very soon; very quickly
- *in order of*: arranged according to
- *in order to*: for the purpose of
- *in part*: to some degree
- *in particular*: especially
- *in power*: (of a political party) holding office
- *in practice*: able to do something well because of recent practice; in reality (opposite of in theory)
- *in print*: (of a book) printed and available from the publisher
- *in private*: not in front of other people

— *in public*: openly; not in private
— *in reality*: really
— *in reserve*: saved for later use
— *in retrospect*: looking back over past events
— *in return for*: as repayment for
— *be in the right*: be correct
— *in season*: (of fruit or vegetables) readily available at that time of year
— *in a second*: soon; quickly
— *in short supply*: scarce; not easily obtainable
— *in sight*: able to be seen
— *in stock*: (of goods at a store) present and available
— *in that case*: if that is true
— *in theory*: ideally; according to theoretical considerations
— *be in time*: not be late
— *in touch with in*: communication with; informed about
— *in triplicate*: so that there are three identical copies (of a document)
— *be in trouble*: be in a difficult situation; be blamed or punished for doing something wrong
— *in tune*: at the correct pitch
— *act in unison*: act together
— *in vain*: without success
— *in the vicinity of*: near

- *once in a while*: occasionally
- *in words of one syllable*: (explain something) clearly and simply
- *in working order*: able to function properly
- *in the wrong*: responsible for an error; guilty

Inside

- *inside out*: with the inner side out; thoroughly

Into

- *PAINT ONESELF INTO A CORNER*: take a course of
- action which greatly narrows one's future
- choices of action
- *go into hiding*: hide oneself
- *get into a rut*: get into a fixed and uninteresting way of life
- *get into trouble*: get into a difficult situation; do something deserving blame or punishment

Of

- *of course*: certainly; as one would expect; as everyone knows
- *hard of hearing*: somewhat deaf
- *next of kin*: nearest relative or relatives
- *of one's own accord*: voluntarily; on one's own initiative
- *of one's own free will*: voluntarily; by choice
- *one's point of view*: one's opinion about

something

- *right of way*: public right to use a path or road; (of road traffic) right to proceed before others
- *rule of thumb*: a simple way to calculate what procedure to follow, based on extensive experience, rather than on theoretical considerations

Off

- *go off the air*: (of radio or television) stop broadcasting
- *off duty*: not engaged in one's regular work
- *off one's hands*: no longer one's responsibility
- *off and on*: from time to time
- *off the record*: say something privately, that is not to be officially recorded
- *off the track*: following a wrong line of thought or action

On

- *on account of*: because of
- *be on the air*: (of radio or television) be in the process of broadcasting
- *on the alert*: ready to act
- *be on all fours*: (of a person) be on hands and knees
- *on the average*: usually; normally
- *on behalf of*: for; in the interests of
- *on board*: on a ship or airplane

— *on business*: as part of one's work
— *on condition that*: only if; provided that
— *on demand*: when asked for
— *on display*: being exhibited
— *on duty*: engaged in one's regular work
— *on fire*: burning
— *to go on foot*: to walk
— *be on one's guard*: be alert and ready to meet an attack
— *on hand*: available
— *ON LOAN*: lent and not yet returned
— *shoot on location*: (of a movie) film in natural surroundings, not in a studio
— *on the lookout*: watchful
— *put something on the map*: cause something to become well-known
— *GET ON ONE'S NERVES*: annoy; irritate
— *on no account*: absolutely not
— *on the one hand*: (used to introduce one side of an argument)
— *on one's own*: alone; without help
— *act on one's own initiative*: act independently, without orders from anyone else
— *on order*: requested but not yet delivered
— *on the other hand*: (used to introduce a contrasting side of an argument)
— *act on principle*: do something to support a

policy

- *on purpose*: deliberately
- *go on record*: say something which is to be officially recorded
- *on sale*: being sold at a lower price than usual
- *on schedule*: at the correct time; as planned or predicted
- *on second thoughts*: after thinking further about something
- *on a shoestring*: with a very small amount of money
- *be on the spot*: be where important events are taking place; be placed in an awkward situation
- *on the spur of the moment*: on a sudden impulse
- *go off on a tangent*: change suddenly to a new line of thought or action
- *on time*: at the correct time
- *walk on tiptoe*: walk on the toes and balls of the feet
- *accept something on trust*: accept something without proof
- *on the verge of*: very close to; about to
- *on the whole*: taking everything into consideration

Out of

- *out of the blue*: unexpectedly
- *out of breath*: (after running) panting from a shortage of oxygen

- *out of character*: unlike a person's known character
- *out of control*: not able to be regulated or guided
- *out of danger*: safe
- *out of date*: no longer used; old-fashioned; (of news) no longer true
- *out of debt*: having paid one's debts
- *be out of one's depth*: be unable to handle a situation because of lack of experience
- *out of doors*: in the open air; not in a building
- *out of fashion*: not fashionable; not presently in common use
- *out of hand*: not under control
- *out of harm's way*: safe
- *out of line with*: in disagreement with
- *be out of one's mind*: be insane
- *out of order*: not functioning properly; (at a formal meeting) not behaving according to the rules
- *out of the ordinary*: unusual
- *out of place*: unsuitable
- *out of practice*: unable to do something as well as one has in past, because of lack of recent practice
- *out of print*: (of a book) no longer available from the publisher
- *out of proportion*: too big or too small; not having the appropriate relationship to something
- *out of the question*: impossible; not to be

considered

- *out of season*: (of fruit or vegetables) not readily available at that time of year
- *out of shape*: (of persons) not in top condition because of lack of exercise
- *out of sight*: hidden, not able to be seen
- *out of stock*: (of goods at a store) temporarily unavailable
- *out of style*: not fashionable
- *out of touch*: with not in communication with; not informed about
- *out of town*: having temporarily left town
- *out of trouble*: not in trouble
- *out of tune*: not at the correct pitch
- *out of work*: no longer having employment

To

- *to all intents and purposes*: in all important ways
- *to a certain extent*: partly
- *to date*: so far; until now
- *up to date*: current; modern
- *see eye to eye with*: agree entirely with
- *take something to heart*: be much affected by something
- *made to measure*: exactly suitable; (of clothes) made for a certain person
- *keep something to oneself*: not tell anyone
- *to the point*: relevant

Under

- *under age*: below the age of being legally permitted to do something
- *be under arrest*: be held prisoner and charged with wrongdoing
- *under the auspices of*: with the patronage of; supported by
- *under one's breath*: in a whisper
- *under the circumstances*: because this is true
- *under consideration*: being thought about
- *under control*: able to be regulated or guided
- *under cover of*: protected by; undetected because of
- *under fire*: being shot at; being criticized
- *under the impression that*: having the idea that
- *be under the influence of*: be affected by
- *be under oath*: have sworn to tell the truth
- *under observation*: being watched carefully
- *under restraint*: prevented from doing something

Up

- *have something up one's sleeve*: have a secret idea or plan in reserve

With

- *with impunity*: without risk of injury or punishment
- *with the naked eye*: without using a magnifying

lens

- *with no strings attached*: (of help given) with no conditions; to be used freely
- *take with a pinch of salt*: not believe completely
- *with regard to*: concerning; about
- *with respect to*: concerning; about
- *tarred with the same brush*: having the same faults
- *with a vengeance*: very much; more than usual

Within

- *within limits*: to a certain extent; not too much
- *within living memory*: within the memory of people now alive

Without

- *go without saying*: be obvious

NOUNS FOLLOWED BY PREPOSITIONS

The following are examples of nouns which are usually followed by certain prepositions. In the case of phrases which are idioms, the meanings of the phrases are indicated in brackets.

Against

take precautions against

For

have affection for

have compassion for

a reason for

make allowances for

an excuse for

have a reputation for

have respect for
have sympathy for
have a talent for
lie in wait for (ambush)
pave the way for (prepare for)

From

absence from

In

have confidence in
have faith in
have an interest in
take part in
make progress in

Into

have insight into

Of

have an abhorrence of
an acknowledgement of
take advantage of
take care of
take command of
evidence of
an example of
an excess of
make a fool of
make fun of (ridicule)
have an impression of
a lack of
neglect of
a number of
a pair of
be part of
a possibility of
make a practice of (do often)
a proof of
a quantity of
recognition of
a recollection of

a result of
run the risk of (risk)
catch sight of
a sign of
a survey of
a symbol of
a symptom of
a token of
make use of
a way of
wash one's hands of (stop caring about and dealing with)

On

an attack on
dependence on
make an impression on
play a joke on
shed light on (explain)
have pity on

To

have access to
pay attention to
an objection to
a reply to
a response to
lay siege to (besiege)
shut one's eyes to (deliberately ignore a problem)

Toward or Towards

animosity toward(s)
an attitude toward(s)

With

have a connection with
find fault with (criticize)
fall in love with
change places with

ADJECTIVES AND VERBS IN THE PASSIVE VOICE

In some cases different prepositions can be used

without causing a change in meaning. For instance, the following examples both have the same meaning.

e.g. I was angry at them.

— I was angry with them.

However, in many cases, the use of different prepositions causes a change in meaning. For instance, the past participle protected is typically followed by the preposition from. However, like many other past participles, protected may also be followed by the preposition by, where by serves to introduce the performer of the action expressed by the past participle.

e.g. The city is protected from the soldiers.

— The city is protected by the soldiers.

The first example indicates that the soldiers are a threat to the city; whereas the second example indicates that the soldiers are protecting the city.

About

anxious about

concerned about

curious about

depressed about

doubtful about

enthusiastic about

excited about

happy about

pleased about

wrong about

worried about

At

adept at

alarmed at

amazed at

overjoyed at

shocked at surprised at

Between

torn between

By

accompanied by caused by
guided by manufactured by
obsessed by written by

For

blamed for eligible for
famous for fit for
known for late for
noted for praised for
punished for qualified for
ready for responsible for
ripe for sorry for
suitable for

From

absent from apart from
derived from descended from
detached from different from
distinct from exempt from
far from isolated from
omitted from protected from
removed from safe from

separated from

In

absorbed in
engaged in
interested in
disappointed in
immersed in
involved in

Of

accused of
ashamed of
capable of
composed of
convinced of
devoid of
ignorant of
jealous of
regardless of
sure of
suspected of
tired of
afraid of
aware of
certain of
conscious of
deprived of
fond of
independent of
proud of
reminded of
suspicious of
terrified of
worthy of

On

based on
intent on
dependent on

To

acceptable to
accustomed to
accessible to
adapted to

addicted to
adjacent to
attached to
attributable to
close to
committed to
comparable to
dedicated to
detrimental to
devoted to
due to
equal to
equivalent to
essential to
exposed to
faithful to
favorable to
foreign to
impervious to
indifferent to
indispensable to
inferior to
kind to
loyal to
next to
obedient to
obliged to
oblivious to
partial to
peculiar to
preferable to
prior to
proportional to
reconciled to
reduced to
related to
relative to
relevant to
resigned to
resistant to
restricted to
senior to
sensitive to
similar to
subject to
subordinate to
suited to
superior to
susceptible to
tied to

Toward or Towards

protective toward(s)

With

acquainted with
affiliated with
associated with
besieged with
compared with
compatible with
confronted with
consistent with
covered with
cursed with
exasperated with
familiar with
finished with
identified with
infatuated with
patient with
pleased with
satisfied with
synonymous with
threatened with

VERBS FOLLOWED BY PREPOSITIONS

The following are examples of verbs which are often followed by certain prepositions.

About

care about
complain about
forget about
lie about (tell a lie)
reminisce about
talk about
think about
wonder about
worry about

Against

discriminate against
protest against
react against
rebel against
turn against

At

aim at
bark at
connive at
frown at
gaze at
glare at
growl at
hint at
look at
point at
shoot at
smile at
snap at
sneer at
stare at
wave at
wink at

For

apply for
apologize for
beg for
blame for
budget for
hope for
long for
look for
mourn for
pay for
plead for
pose for
pray for
prepare for
press for
register for
search for
shop for
substitute for
vouch for
wait for
wish for

From

abstain from	benefit from
deduct from	derive from
desist from	deter from
detract from	deviate from
differ from	divert from
escape from	extricate from
flee from	infer from
profit from	protect from
quote from	radiate from
recoil from	recover from
refrain from	shrink from
stem from	suffer from

In

believe in	engage in
indulge in	intervene in
invest in	participate in
persist in	succeed in

Into

change into	convert into
delve into	dip into
develop into	divide into
fall into	merge into
plunge into	pry into
sink into	transform into

Of

approve of	beware of
conceive of	consist of
deprive of	die of
disapprove of	smell of

On

blame on	concentrate on
depend on	impinge on
impose on	insist on
intrude on	pounce on
reflect on	rely on
report on	spy on
subsist on	thrive on

Over

preside over	trip over

To

adapt to	adhere to
adjust to	amount to
belong to	conform to
contribute to	correspond to
listen to	object to
pertain to	prefer to
refer to	relate to
respond to	resort to

revert to
submit to
subscribe to
succumb to
surrender to
yield to

With

agree with
associate with
collaborate with
combine with
communicate with
comply with
concur with
consort with
contend with
cooperate with
cope with
correspond with
flirt with
mingle with
share with
sympathize with

2

Preposition and Postposition

In English, the most used prepositions are "of", "to", "in", "for", and "on". Simply put, a preposition indicates a relation between things mentioned in a sentence. Linguists sometimes distinguish between a preposition, which precedes its phrase, a postposition, which follows its phrase, and as a rare case a circumposition, which surrounds its phrase. Taken together, these three parts of speech are called adpositions.

In more technical language, an adposition is an element that, prototypically, combines syntactically with a phrase and indicates how that phrase should be interpreted in the surrounding context. Some linguists use the word "preposition" instead of "adposition" for all three cases.

In linguistics, adpositions are considered to be members of the syntactic category "P". "PPs", consisting of an adpositional head and its complement phrase, are used for a wide range of syntactic and semantic functions, most commonly modification and complementation. The following examples illustrate some uses of English prepositional phrases:

- as a modifier to a verb
  - sleep throughout the winter
  - danced atop the tables for hours
- as a modifier to a noun
  - the weather in April
  - cheeses from France with live bacteria
- as the complement of a verb
  - insist on staying home
  - dispose of unwanted items
- as the complement of a noun
  - a thirst for revenge
  - an amendment to the constitution
- as the complement of an adjective or adverb
  - attentive to their needs
  - separately from its neighbours
- as the complement of another preposition
  - until after supper
  - from beneath the bed

Adpositions perform many of the same functions as case markings, but adpositions are syntactic elements, while case markings are morphological elements.

Adpositions form a heterogeneous class, with fuzzy boundaries that tend to overlap with other categories (like verbs, nouns, and adjectives). It is thus impossible to provide an absolute definition that picks out all and only the adpositions in every language. The following features, however, are often required of adpositions.

- An adposition combines syntactically with exactly one complement phrase, most often a noun phrase (or, in a different analysis, a determiner phrase). In English, this is generally a noun (or something functioning as a noun, e.g., a gerund), called the object of the preposition, together with its attendant modifiers.
- An adposition establishes the grammatical relationship that links its complement phrase to another word or phrase in the context. In English, it also establishes a semantic relationship, which may be spatial (in, on, under,...), temporal (after, during,...), or logical (via,...) in nature.
- An adposition determines certain grammatical properties of its complement (e.g. its case). In English, the objects of prepositions are always in the objective case. In Koine Greek, certain prepositions always take their objects in a certain case, and other prepositions may take their object in one of several cases, depending on the meaning of the preposition.
- Adpositions are non-inflecting (or "invariant"); i.e., they do not have paradigms of forms (for different tenses, cases, genders, etc.) in the same way as verbs, adjectives, and nouns in the same language. There are exceptions, though, for example in Celtic languages.

PROPERTIES

The following properties are characteristic of most adpositional systems.

- Adpositions are among the most frequently occurring words in languages that have them.

For example, one frequency ranking for English word forms begins as follows (adpositions in bold):

the, of, and, to, a, in, that, it, is, was, I, for, on, you, ...

- The most common adpositions are single, monomorphemic words. According to the ranking cited above, for example, the most common English prepositions are:

of, to, in, for, on, with, as, by, at, from, ...

- Adpositions form a closed class of lexical items and cannot be productively derived from words of other categories.

PREPOSITION STRANDING

Preposition stranding, sometimes called "P-stranding", is the syntactic construction in which a preposition appears without an object. (The preposition is then described as "stranded" or "hanging".) This construction is widely found in Germanic languages, including English and the North Germanic languages (Swedish, Danish, Norwegian, Icelandic); whether or not German and Dutch exhibit legitimate preposition stranding is debatable.

P-stranding is also found in languages outside the Germanic family, such as Vata and Gbadi, two languages in the Niger-Congo family, and certain dialects of French spoken in North America. In English, some grammarians frown upon preposition stranding.

TYPES OF PREPOSITIONS

Adpositions can be organised into subclasses according to various criteria. These can be based on directly observable properties (such as the adposition's form or its position in the sentence) or on less visible properties (such as the adposition's meaning or function in the context at hand).

Simple and Complex

Simple adpositions consist of a single word, while complex adpositions consist of a group of words that act as one unit. Some examples of complex prepositions in English are:

> in spite of, with respect to, except for, by dint of, next to

The boundary between simple and complex adpositions is not clear-cut. Many simple adpositions are derived from complex forms through grammaticalisation. This change takes time, and during the transitional stages the adposition acts in some ways like a single word, and in other ways like a multi-word unit. For example, current German orthographic conventions recognise the indeterminate status of the following adpositions, allowing two spellings:

— anstelle / an Stelle ("instead of"), aufgrund / auf Grund ("because of"), mithilfe / mit Hilfe ("thanks to"), zugunsten / zu Gunsten ("in favour of"), zuungunsten / zu Ungunsten ("to the disadvantage of"), zulasten / zu Lasten ("at the expense of")

The boundary between complex adpositions and free combinations of words is also a fuzzy one. For English, this involves structures of the form "preposition + (article) + noun + preposition". Many sequences in English, such as in front of, that are traditionally regarded as prepositional phrases are not so regarded by linguists. The following characteristics are good indications that a given combination is "frozen" enough to be considered a complex preposition in English:

- It contains a word that cannot be used in any other context: by dint of, in lieu of.
- The first preposition cannot be replaced: with a view to but not for/without a view to
- It is impossible to insert an article, or to use a different article: on an/the account of, for the/ a sake of
- The range of possible adjectives is very limited: in great favour of, but not in helpful favour of
- The number of the noun cannot be changed: by virtue/ virtues of
- It is impossible to use a possessive determiner: in spite of him, not in his spite

Complex prepositions develop through the grammaticalisation of commonly-used free combinations. This is an ongoing process that introduces new prepositions into English.

Classification by Position

The surface position of an adposition with respect to its complement allows us to define the following subclasses:

- A preposition precedes its complement to form a prepositional phrase.

  German: auf dem Tisch, French: sur la table, Polish: na stole ("on the table")

- A postposition follows its complement to form a postpositional phrase.

These two terms are in fact much more commonly used than the more general adposition. Whether a language has primarily prepositions or postpositions is seen as an important aspect of its typological classification, correlated with many other properties of the language according to research into linguistic universals.

It is usually straightforward to say whether an adposition precedes or follows its complement, but in some cases, the complement may not appear in its "normal" position. For example, in preposition stranding constructions, the complement appears somewhere to the left of the preposition:

- {How much money} did you say the guy wanted to sell us the car for?
- She's going to the Bahamas? {Who} with?

In other cases, the complement of the adposition is missing altogether:

- I'm going to the park. Do you want to come with?
- French: Il fait trop froid, je ne suis pas habillée pour. ("It's too cold, I'm not dressed for [this situation].")

The adpositions in these examples are generally still considered to be prepositions, because when they form a phrase with the complement (in more ordinary constructions), they must appear first.

Some adpositions can in fact appear on either side of their complement; these might be called ambipositions:

- He slept {through the whole night}/{the whole night through}.
- German: {meiner Meinung nach}/{nach meiner Meinung} ("in my opinion")

An ambiposition may have distinct meanings, and it may govern distinct cases, depending on its position. Another logical possibility is for the adposition to appear on both sides of its complement:

- A circumposition has two parts, which surround the complement to form a circumpositional phrase.
  - English: from now on
  - Dutch: naar het einde toe ("to the end", lit. "to the end to")
  - French: a un detail pres ("except for one detail", lit. "at one detail near")

"Circumposition" can be useful as a descriptive term, although on closer inspection, most circumpositional phrases can be broken down into a more hierarchical structure, or given a different analysis altogether.

For example, the Mandarin example above could be analysed as a prepositional phrase headed by cong ("from"), taking the postpositional phrase bingxiang li ("refrigerator inside") as its complement. Alternatively, the cong may be analysed as not being a preposition at all.

— An inposition is an adposition between constituents of a complex complement.
— Ambiposition is a term sometimes used for an adposition that can function as either a preposition or a postposition.

Melis proposes the descriptive term interposition for adpositions in the structures such as the following:

— mot a mot ("word for word"), coup sur coup ("one after another, repeatedly"), page apres page ("page upon page")

These phrases do require special attention, but the term "interposition" cannot be taken literally to mean that the adposition appears inside its complement (because the two nouns do not form a single phrase mot mot or page page). Genuine examples of "interposed" adpositions can be found in Latin (e.g. summa cum laude, lit. "highest with praise"), but these are always related to a more basic prepositional structure.

COMPLEMENT CLASSIFICATION

Although noun phrases are the most typical complements, adpositions can in fact combine with a variety of syntactic categories, much like verbs.

— noun phrases: It was on {the table}.
— adpositional phrases: Come out from {under the bed}.
— adjectives and adjective phrases: The scene went from {blindingly bright} to {pitch black}.
— adverb or adverb phrases: I worked there until recently

- infinitival or participial verb phrases: Let's think about solving this problem.
- interrogative clauses: we can't agree on {whether to have children or not}
- full sentences

Also like verbs, adpositions can appear without a complement. Some adpositions could be described as combining with two complements:

- {With Sammy president}, we can all come out of hiding again.
- {For Sammy to become president}, they'd have to seriously modify the Constitution.

It is more commonly assumed, however, that Sammy and the following predicate first forms a small clause, which then becomes the single complement of the preposition.

SEMANTIC CLASSIFICATION

Adpositions can be used to express a wide range of semantic relations between their complement and the rest of the context. The following list is not an exhaustive classification:

- spatial relations: location (inclusion, exclusion, proximity), direction (origin, path, endpoint)
- temporal relations
- comparison: equality, opposition, price, rate
- content: source, material, subject matter
- instrument, manner
- cause, purpose, agent

Most common adpositions are highly polysemous, and much research is devoted to the description and explanation of the various interconnected meanings of particular adpositions. In many cases a primary, spatial meaning can be identified, which is then extended to non-spatial uses by metaphorical or other processes.

In some contexts, adpositions appear in contexts where their semantic contribution is minimal, perhaps altogether absent. Such adpositions are sometimes referred to as functional or case-marking adpositions, and they are lexically selected by another element in the construction, or fixed by the construction as a whole.

- English: dispense with formalities, listen to my advice, good at mathematics
- Russian: otvechat' na vopros (lit. "answer on the question"), obvinenie v obmane ("accusation in [i.e. of] fraud")
- Spanish: sonar con ganar el titulo ("dream with [i.e. about] winning the title"), consistir en dos grupos ("consist in [i.e. of] two groups")

It is usually possible to find some semantic motivation for the choice of a given adposition, but it is generally impossible to explain why other semantically motivated adpositions are excluded in the same context. The selection of the correct adposition in these cases is a matter of syntactic well-formedness.

Subclasses of spatial adpositions

Spatial adpositions can be divided into two main classes, namely directional and static ones. A directional adposition usually involves motion along a path over time, but can also denote a non-temporal path. Examples of directional adpositions include to, from, towards, into, along and through.

— Bob went to the store. (movement over time)

— a path into the woods (non-temporal path)

— The fog extended from London to Paris (non-temporal path)

A static adposition normally does not involve movement. Examples of these include at, in, on, beside, behind, under and above.

— Bob is at the store.

Directional adpositions differ from static ones in that they normally can't combine with a copula to yield a predicate, though there are some exceptions to this, as in Bob is from Australia, which may perhaps be thought of as special uses.

— Fine: Bob is in his bedroom. (in is static)

— Bad: Bob is to his bedroom. (to is directional)

Directional spatial adpositions can only combine with verbs that involve motion; static prepositions can combine with other verbs as well.

— Fine: Bob is lying down in his bedroom.

— Bad: Bob is lying down into/from his bedroom.

When a static adposition combines with a motion verb, it sometimes takes on a directional meaning. The following sentence can either mean that Bob jumped around in the water, or else that he jumped so that he ended up in the water.

— Bob jumped in the water.

In some languages, directional adpositions govern a different case on their complement than static ones.

For example, in German, directional adpositions govern accusative while static ones govern dative. Adpositions that are ambiguous between directional and static interpretations govern accusative when they are interpreted as directional, and dative when they are interpreted as static.

– in seinem Zimmer (in his-DATIVE room) "in his room" (static)
– in sein Zimmer (in his-ACCUSATIVE room) "into his room" (directional)

Directional adpositions can be further divided into telic ones and atelic ones. To, into and across are telic: they involve movement all the way to the endpoint denoted by their complement. Atelic ones include towards and along. When telic adpositions combine with a motion verb, the result is a telic verb phrase. Atelic adpositions give rise to atelic verb phrases when so combined.

Static adpositions can be further subdivided into projective and non-projective ones. A non-projective static adposition is one whose meaning can be determined by inspecting the meaning of its complement and the meaning of the preposition itself. A projective static adposition requires, in addition, a perspective or point of view. If I say that Bob is behind the rock you need to know where I am in order to know on which side of the rock Bob is supposed to be. If I say that your pen is to the left of my book you also need to know what my point of view is. No such point of view is required in the interpretation of sentences like your pen is on the desk. Projective static prepositions can sometimes take the complement itself as "point of view," if this provides us with certain information. For example, a house normally has a front and a back, so a sentence like the following is actually ambiguous between two readings: one has it that Bob is at the back of the house; the other has it that Bob is on the other side of the house, with respect to the speaker's point of view.

Bob is behind the house.

A similar effect can be observed with left of, given that objects that have fronts and backs can also be ascribed lefts and rights. The sentence, My keys are to the left of the phone, can either mean that they are on the speaker's left of the phone, or on the phone's left of the phone.

Particular uses of adpositions can be classified according to the function of the adpositional phrase in the sentence.

- Modification
  - adverb-like
    - The athlete ran {across the goal line}.
  - adjective-like
    - attributively
      - A road trip {with children} is not the most relaxing vacation.
    - in the predicate position
      - The key is {under the plastic rock}.
- Syntactic functions
  - complement

— Let's dispense with the formalities.

Here the words dispense and with complement one another, functioning as a unit to mean forego, and they share the direct object (the formalities). The verb dispense would not have this meaning without the word with to complement it.

— subject (impossible in many languages)

{In the cellar} was chosen as the best place to hide the bodies.

— object of the verb (rare or impossible in English, but very common e.g. in Koine Greek)

Adpositional languages typically single out a particular adposition for the following special functions:

- marking possession
- marking the agent in the passive construction
- marking the beneficiary role in transfer relations

OVERLAPS WITH OTHER CATEGORIES

Adverbs

We observe many similarities in form between adpositions and adverbs. Some adverbs are transparently derived from the fusion of a preposition and its complement, and some prepositions have adverb-like uses with no complement:

- {down the stairs}/downstairs, {under the ground}/underground.
- {inside (the house)}, {aboard (the plane)}, {underneath (the surface)}

It is possible to treat all of these adverbs as intransitive prepositions, as opposed to transitive prepositions, which select a complement (just like transitive vs intransitive verbs). This analysis could also be extended to other adverbs, even those that cannot be used as "ordinary" prepositions with a nominal complement:

- here, there, abroad, downtown, astray, ...
- today, tomorrow, yesterday, soon, afterwards, someday, ...
- recently, carefully, honestly, ...

A more conservative approach is to say simply that adverbs and adpositional phrases share many common functions. Phrasal verbs in English are composed of a verb and a "particle" that also looks like an intransitive preposition. The same can be said for the separable verb prefixes found in Dutch (and German).

- give up, look out, sleep in, carry on, come to
- Dutch: opbellen ("call up"), aanbieden ("offer"), voorstellen ("present")

Although these elements have the same lexical form as prepositions, in many cases they do not have relational semantics, and there is no "missing" complement whose identity can be recovered from the context.

Conjunctions

The set of adpositions overlaps with the set of subordinating conjunctions (or complementisers):

— (preposition) before/after/since the end of the summer

— (conjunction) before/after/since the summer ended

— It looks like another rainy day (preposition) / it's going to rain again today (conjunction).

All of these words can be treated as prepositions if we extend the definition to allow clausal complements. This treatment could be extended further to conjunctions that are never used as ordinary prepositions:

— unless they surrender, although time is almost up, while you were on the phone

Coverbs

In some languages, the role of adpositions is served by coverbs, words that are lexically verbs, but are generally used to convey the meaning of adpositions. For instance, whether prepositions exist in Chinese is sometimes considered an open question. Coverbs are often referred to as prepositions because they appear before the noun phrase they modify. However, unlike prepositions, coverbs can sometimes stand alone as main verbs.

Case Affixes

From a functional point of view, adpositions and morphological case markings are strikingly similar. An adpositional phrase in one language often corresponds directly to a case-marked noun phrase in another language. For example, the agentive noun phrase in the passive construction in English is introduced by the preposition by, while in Russian it is marked by the instrumental case: "cy", "om", or "ami", depending on the noun's gender and number. Sometimes both prepositions and cases can be observed within a single language.

For example, in certain uses the genitive case in German is interchangeable with a von prepositional phrase.

Despite this functional similarity, adpositions and case markings are distinct grammatical categories:

— Adpositions combine syntactically with their complement phrase. Case markings combine with a noun morphologically.

— Two adpositions can usually be joined with a conjunction and share a single complement, but this is normally not possible with case markings:

  {of and for the people} vs. Latin populi et populo, not populi et -o ("people-genitive and -dative")

— One adposition can usually combine with two coordinated complements, but this is normally not possible with case markings:

  of {the city and the world} vs. Latin urbis et orbis, not urb- et orbis ("city and world-genitive ")

— Case markings combine primarily with nouns, whereas adpositions can combine with phrases of many different categories.

- A case marking usually appears directly on the noun, but an adposition can be separated from the noun by other words.
- Within the noun phrase, determiners and adjectives may agree with the noun in case (case spreading), but an adposition only appears once.
- A language can have hundreds of adpositions (including complex adpositions), but no language has this many distinct morphological cases.

Still, it can be difficult to draw a clear boundary between case markings and adpositions. For example, the post-nominal elements in Japanese and Korean are sometimes called case particles and sometimes postpositions. Sometimes they are analysed as two different groups because they have different characteristics (e.g. ability to combine with focus particles), but in such analysis, it is unclear which words should fall into which group.

Turkish and Finnish have both extensive case-marking and postpositions, and here there is evidence to help distinguish the two:

- Turkish: (case) sinemaya (cinema-dative, "to the cinema ") vs (postposition) sinema için ("for the cinema")
- Finnish: (case) talossa (house-inessive, "in the house") vs (postposition) "talon edessä (house-gen in-front, "in front of the house")

In these examples, the case markings form a word with their hosts (as shown by vowel harmony, other word-internal effects and agreement of adjectives in Finnish), while the postpositions are independent words. In Indo-European languages, each case often contains several different endings, some of which may even be derived from different roots. An ending is chosen depending on gender, number, whether the word is a noun or a modifier, and other factors.

WORD CHOICE

In ambiguous cases, there is not always a clear rule which adposition is appropriate, and different languages and regional dialects may have different conventions. Learning the conventionally preferred word is a matter of exposure to examples. For example, most dialects of American English have "to wait in line", but some have "to wait on line". It is for this reason that prepositions are one of the most difficult aspects of a language to learn for non-native speakers.

In some cases, the preposition is not translated from one language into another, and is thus omitted. Those learning English may have difficulty distinguishing between the prepositions on, in, and at, as other languages may use only one or two prepositions for the equivalent of three in English. On the other hand, speakers of English learning Spanish or Portuguese have difficulty distinguishing between the prepositions por and para, as both frequently mean for in English.

3

List of English Prepositions

In English, some prepositions are short, typically containing five letters or fewer. There are, however, a significant number of multi-word prepositions. Throughout the history of the English language, new prepositions have come into use, old ones fallen out of use, and the meaning of existing prepositions changed. Nonetheless, the prepositions are by and large a closed class.

SINGLE WORDS

abaft	aboard
about	above
absent	across
after	against
along	alongside
amid	amidst
among	amongst
around	as
aslant	astride
at	athwart

atop	barring
before	behind
below	beneath
beside	besides
between	beyond
but	by
concerning	despite
down	during
except	failing
following	for
from	in
inside	into
like	mid (from "amid". Usually used poetically.)
minus	near
next	notwithstanding (also used postpositionally)
of	off
on	onto
opposite	out
outside	over
past	per
plus	regarding
round	save
since	than

through	throughout
till	times
to	toward
towards	under
underneath	unlike
until	up
upon	via
with	within
without	worth

MULTI WORDS

Two Words

according to	ahead of
aside from	because of
close to	due to
except for	far from
in to	inside of
instead of	near to
next to	on to (contracted as onto)
out from	out of
outside of	owing to
prior to	pursuant to
regardless of	subsequent to

Three Words

as far as	as well as

by means of	in accordance with
in addition to	in case of
in front of	in lieu of
in place of	in spite of
on account of	on behalf of
on top of	

INFREQUENTLY USED

anent	anti (loan word)
behither	betwixt
circa (loan word)	cum (loan word)
in lieu of (loan word)	pro (loan word)
qua (loan word)	re (loan word)
sans (loan word)	unto (largely supplanted by to; used in some formal, religious, and/or archaic contexts)
versus (loan word)	vis-a-vis (loan word)

NOT FULLY GRAMMATICALIZED

concerning
considering
regarding

QUANTIFIED NOUN PHRASES

apart from	but
except	plus

4

Place Prepositions

Prepositions of place are used to clarify a specific place. Place prepositions are used with all nouns. The preposition usually comes before the noun or the pronoun. The preposition never comes before a verb.

In general, we use:

— at for a point
— in for an enclosed space
— on for a surface

at	in	on
point	enclosed space	surface
at the corner	in the garden	on the wall
at the bus stop	in London	on the ceiling
at the door	in France	on the door
at the top of the page	in a box	on the cover
at the end of the road	in my pocket	on the floor
at the entrance	in my wallet	on the carpet
at the crossroads	in a building	on the menu
at the entrance	in a car	on a page

Look at these examples:

- Jane is waiting for you at the bus stop.
- The shop is at the end of the street.
- My plane stopped at Dubai and Hanoi and arrived in Bangkok two hours late.
- When will you arrive at the office?
- Do you work in an office?
- I have a meeting in New York.
- Do you live in Japan?
- Jupiter is in the Solar System.
- The author's name is on the cover of the book.
- There are no prices on this menu.
- You are standing on my foot.
- There was a "no smoking" sign on the wall.
- I live on the 7th floor at 21 Oxford Street in London.

Notice the use of the prepositions of place at, in and on in these standard expressions:

at	in	on
at home	in a car	on a bus
at work	in a taxi	on a train
at school	in a helicopter	on a plane
at university	in a boat	on a ship
at college	in a lift (elevator)	on a bicycle,
at the top	in the newspaper	on a horse, on an elephant
at the bottom	in the sky	on the radio, on television

at the side	in a row	on the left, on the right
at reception	in Oxford Street	on the way

COMMON PLACE PREPOSITIONS

— aboard - She is aboard the boat.

— above - The picture is above the sofa.

— across - My house is across the street.

— against - The desk is against the wall.

— around - My house is around the block.

— at - Is your house at the end of the street.

— at the back of - We are going to sit at the back of the theater.

— at the bottom of - The coins are at the bottom of the lake.

— at the top of - The books are at the top of the shelves.

— between - We sit between the two boys.

— behind - The girls sit behind the two boys.

— below - The desk is below the window

— by - The books are by the door.

— in - I live in the big green and white house.

— inside - I live inside the big green house.

— on the corner of - We live on the corner of 3rd avenue

— in the middle of - We live in the middle of the street.

— near - I don't live near the supermarket.

- next to - I live next to my best friend.
- to the left of - The blue box is to the left of the green box.
- to the right of - The orange box is to the right of the yellow box.
- on - The sun heater is on the top of the building.
- on the side of - There is a big sign on the side of the house.
- on top of - There is a man on the top of the roof.
- on the other side of - Do you see what is going on over there on the other side of the roof?
- opposite - The post office is on the opposite side of the street.
- outside - The car is outside the garage.
- under - The blanket is under the bed in a box..
- underneath - The pen is underneath the box.

5

Preposition of Time: at, in, on

We use:

— at for a precise time

— in for months, years, centuries and long periods

— on for days and dates

at	in	on
Precise Time	Months, Years, Centuries and Long periods	Days and Dates
at 3 o'clock	in May	on Sunday
at 10.30am	in summer	on Tuesdays
at noon	in the summer	on 6 March
at dinnertime	in 1990	on 25 Dec. 2010
at bedtime	in the 1990s	on Christmas Day
at sunrise	in the next century	on Independence Day
at sunset	in the Ice Age	on my birthday
at the moment	in the past/future	on New Year's Eve

Look at these examples:

- I have a meeting at 9am.
- The shop closes at midnight.
- Jane went home at lunchtime.
- In England, it often snows in December.
- Do you think we will go to Jupiter in the future?
- There should be a lot of progress in the next century.
- Do you work on Mondays?
- Her birthday is on 20 November.
- Where will you be on New Year's Day?

Notice the use of the preposition of time at in the following standard expressions:

Expression	Example
at night	The stars shine at night.
at the weekend	I don't usually work at the weekend.
at Christmas/Easter	I stay with my family at Christmas.
at the same time	We finished the test at the same time.
at present	He's not home at present. Try later.

Notice the use of the prepositions of time in and on in these common expressions:

in	on
in the morning	on Tuesday morning
in the mornings	on Saturday mornings

in the afternoon(s)	on Sunday afternoons
in the evening(s)	on Monday evening

When we say last, next, every, this we do not also use at, in, on.

- I went to London last June. (not in last June)
- He's coming back next Tuesday. (noton next Tuesday)
- I go home every Easter. (not at every Easter)
- We'll call you this evening. (not in this evening)

ONE POINT IN TIME

On is used with days:

- I will see you on Monday.7
- The week begins on Sunday.

At is used with noon, night, midnight, and with the time of day:

- My plane leaves at noon.
- The movie starts at 6 p.m.

In is used with other parts of the day, with months, with years, with seasons:

- He likes to read in the afternoon.
- The days are long in August.
- The book was published in 1999.
- The flowers will bloom in spring.

EXTENDED TIME

To express extended time, English uses the following

prepositions: since, for, by, from-to, from-until, during,(with)in

- She has been gone since yesterday. (She left yesterday and has not returned.)
- I'm going to Paris for two weeks. (I will spend two weeks there.)
- The movie showed from August to October. (Beginning in August and ending in October.)
- The decorations were up from spring until fall. (Beginning in spring and ending in fall.)
- I watch TV during the evening. (For some period of time in the evening.)
- We must finish the project within a year. (No longer than a year.)

PLACE

To express notions of place, English uses the following prepositions: to talk about the point itself: in, to express something contained: inside, to talk about the surface: on, to talk about a general vicinity, at. For more detail, see our handouts on Prepositions of Location and Prepositions of Direction.

- There is a wasp in the room.
- Put the present inside the box.
- I left your keys on the table.
- She was waiting at the corner.

HIGHER THAN A POINT

To express notions of an object being higher than a point, English uses the following prepositions: over, above. For more detail, see our handout on Prepositions of Spatial Relationship.

– He threw the ball over the roof.

– Hang that picture above the couch.

LOWER THAN A POINT

To express notions of an object being lower than a point, English uses the following prepositions: under, underneath, beneath, below. For more detail, see our handout on Prepositions of Spatial Relationship.

– The rabbit burrowed under the ground.

– The child hid underneath the blanket.

– We relaxed in the shade beneath the branches.

– The valley is below sea-level.

CLOSE TO A POINT

To express notions of an object being close to a point, English uses the following prepositions: near, by, next to, between, among, opposite. For more detail, see our handout on Prepositions of Spatial Relationship.

– She lives near the school.

– There is an ice cream shop by the store.

– An oak tree grows next to my house

– The house is between Elm Street and Maple Street.

– I found my pen lying among the books.

– The bathroom is opposite that room.

TO INTRODUCE OBJECTS OF VERBS

English uses the following prepositions to introduce objects of the following verbs.

- At: glance, laugh, look, rejoice, smile, stare
  - She took a quick glance at her reflection.

    (exception with mirror: She took a quick glance in the mirror.)
  - You didn't laugh at his joke.
  - I'm looking at the computer monitor.
  - We rejoiced at his safe rescue.
  - That pretty girl smiled at you.
  - Stop staring at me.
- Of: approve, consist, smell
  - I don't approve of his speech.
  - My contribution to the article consists of many pages.
  - He came home smelling of alcohol.
- Of (or about): dream, think
  - I dream of finishing college in four years.
  - Can you think of a number between one and ten?
  - I am thinking about this problem.
- For: call, hope, look, wait, watch, wish
  - Did someone call for a taxi?
  - He hopes for a raise in salary next year.
  - I'm looking for my keys.
  - We'll wait for her here.

– You go buy the tickets and I'll watch for the train.

– If you wish for an "A" in this class, you must work hard.

Preposition	Use	Examples
in	in months year	in July; in September in 1985; in 1999
	seasons summer of 69	in summer; in the
	part of the day	in the morning; in the aftererrnoon; in the evening
	duration	in a minute; in two weeks
at	part of the day	at night
	time of day	at 6 o'clock; at midnight
	celebrations	at Christmas; at Easter
	fixed phrases	at the same time
on	days of the week	on Sunday; on Friday
	date	on the 25th of December*
	special holidays	on Good Friday; on Easter Sunday; on my birthday
after	later than sth.	after school
ago	how far sth happend (in the past)	
before	earlier than sth.	before Christmas

between	time that separates two points	between Monday and Friday
by	not later than a special time	by Thursday
during	through the whole of a period of time	during the holidays
for	period of time	for three weeks
from ... to		from Monday to Wednesday
from...	two points form	from Monday till Wednesday
till/until	a period	from Monday until Wednesday
past	time of the day	23 minutes past 6 (6:23)
since	point of time	since Monday
to	time of the day	23 minutes to 6 (5:37)
up to	not more than a special time	up to 6 hours a day
within	during a period of time	within a day

6

Phrasal verbs followed by Preposition

A phrasal verb is an idiom which consists of a verb followed by a preposition, a verb followed by an adverb, or a verb followed by an adverb, followed by a preposition. The phrasal verbs in the following examples are printed in bold type.

e.g. I ran into an old friend.

— We put off washing the dishes.

— They all look up to him.

In these examples, the phrasal verb to run into consists of the verb to run followed by the preposition into, the phrasal verb to put off consists of the verb to put followed by the adverb off, and the phrasal verb to look up to consists of the verb to look followed by the adverb up, followed by the preposition to.

Many phrasal verbs are used more often in informal English than in formal English. In most cases, the ideas expressed by such phrasal verbs may also be expressed by other phrases which are more likely to be used in formal English. For instance in the table below, the phrasal verbs used in the preceding examples are listed in the left-hand column and other phrases with the same meanings are listed in the right-hand column.

Informal	*Formal*
to run into	to meet unexpectedly
to put off	to postpone
to look up to	to admire

It should be noted that the use of many phrasal verbs varies among the different dialects of English. For instance, in order to express the idea of contacting someone by means of the telephone, the expression to ring someone up is frequently used in British English; whereas the expression to call someone is frequently used in American English.

Because of differences in dialect, the forms of the verbs and the meanings given may vary from one dictionary to another. In addition, some phrasal verbs have more than one meaning.

VERB FOLLOWED BY A PREPOSITION

Some phrasal verbs consist of a verb followed by a preposition. A However, in the case of a phrasal verb, the verb followed by the preposition forms an expression with an idiomatic meaning.

For instance, the phrasal verb to come across is an idiomatic expression with the meaning to find. Similarly, the phrasal verb to frown on is an idiomatic expression with the meaning to disapprove of.

e.g. We came across an old diary while we were cleaning out the attic.

— The workers frowned on the practice of smoking in the office.

It should be noted that some phrasal verbs consisting of a verb followed by a preposition can be used in the Passive Voice.

e.g. The practice of smoking in the office was frowned on by the workers.

— The children were looked after by their aunt.

In these examples, the phrasal verbs to frown on and to look after are used in the Passive Voice. The following are examples of phrasal verbs which consist of a verb followed by a preposition. Each phrasal verb is followed by its meaning and an example of its use.

Verbs Followed by Prepositions

abide by: adhere to	We abided by the rules.
account for: explain	He accounted for the discrepancy.
ask for: request	They asked for an exte-nsion.
bank on: depend on	We are banking on good weather tomorrow.
bear with: be patient with	Please bear with the delay.
border on: be near,	Their excitement bordered on hysteria.
break into: enter by force	Thieves broke into the store.
build on: develop from	We want to build on our success.
burst into: suddenly enter	He burst into the room.
call for: demand	This calls for an investigation.
call on: ask, order	We will call on you to give a speech.
come across: find accidentally	She came across some old papers.

come upon: discover	We came upon a small lake.
confide in: share a secret	The two friends confided in each other.
count on: depend on	We are counting on you.
cut across: use a short route	I cut across the parking lot.
dawn on: realise	Finally the truth dawned on him.
deal in: stock, sell	He deals in gold and jewels.
deal with: handle successfully	She can deal with any situation.
decide on: settle on	They decided on a course of action.
dispense with: proceed without	The chairman dispensed with formalities.
dispose of: get rid of	If he moves, he will have to dispose of his furniture.
dwell on: emphasize	He dwelt on the risks involved.
enlarge on: say more about	Please enlarge on your proposal.
enter into: begin, commence	The brothers entered into an agreement.
expand on: say more about	Please expand on what you said before.
frown on: disapprove of	Absenteeism is frowned on.
get at: reach	The store was so crowded, it was hard to get at the food.
get into:become involved with	Idon't want to get into an argument.
get over: recover from	Have you got over the flu yet?
get through: survive, finish	I don't know how I can get through all this work.
go against: oppose	Don't go against the rules.
go over: review	I would like to go over the report again.
go through:examine in detail	Have you gone through the evidence?
go with: look good with	Those shoes don't go with that outfit.

grow on:become more attractive	I'm sure the idea will grow on you.
guard against: take precautions	We must guard against possible attack.
hinge on: depend on	Everything hinges on her decision.
inquire into: investigate	Please inquire into the alternatives.
keep to: adhere to	The train will keep to the schedule.
laugh at: mock, make fun of	Don't laugh at me!
launch into: start	He launched into an explanation.
leaf through: turn the pages	She leafed idly through the book.
live on: survive using	What did you live on?
look after: take care of	I will look after the children.
look into: investigate	He will look into the situation.
look through: examine quickly	We looked through the magazines while we were waiting.
part with:give up reluctantly	She refused to part with her necklace.
pick on: be unkind to	Because he was the youngest, the other boys picked on him.
prey on: hunt and eat; disturb	Ospreys prey on fish; the idea preys on my mind.
provide for: prepare for	We have provided for any emergency.
reason with: try to persuade	It is hard to reason with an angry person.
reckon on: calculate on	I hadn't reckoned on being the center of attention.
rise above: be superior to	He rose above his circumstances and managed to succeed.
run across: find accidentally	They ran across some interesting information.
run into: meet accidentally	I ran into my cousin downtown.
run over: injured by a vehicle	Children must be careful not to be run over by cars.

see through:not be deceived by	I instantly saw through the disguise.
send for: ask to be sent	You will have to send for your transcripts.
settle for: reluctantly accept	Since there was no kale, we had to settle for cabbage.
side with:support in a dispute	Why did you side with him?
sit through: sit and endure	It was all I could do to sit through the lecture without falling asleep.
stand by: support	I hope you will stand by me.
stand for: represent	What does the abbreviation etc. stand for?
stick to: adhere to	We shall stick to the original plan.
stumble across:find accidentally	He stumbled across an interesting fossil.
survive on: survive using	During the winter, we had to survive on turnips and parsnips.
take after: resemble an ancestor	He takes after his grandfather.
tamper with: interfere with	Someone has tampered with the lock.
touch on: mention	She touched on many important subjects.
verge on: approach	His behavior verges on rudeness.
wade through: slowly peruse	We had to wade through a pile of documents.
watch over: guard	The shepherd watched over the sheep.

Position of the Object of the Preposition

The object of a preposition usually follows the preposition, whether the object is a noun or a pronoun. In the following examples, the objects are underlined.

e.g. We have launched into a new project.

– We have launched into it.

In these examples, the noun project and the pronoun it are the objects of the preposition into of the phrasal verb to launch into. Both the noun object and the pronoun object follow the preposition.

Adverbs of Manner

If a verb is followed by a preposition, an adverb of manner may be placed between the verb and the preposition. In the following examples, the adverbs of manner are underlined.

e.g. We reasoned patiently with the little girl.

— I leafed quickly through the book.

In the first example, the adverb of manner patiently is placed between the verb reasoned and the preposition with of the phrasal verb to reason with. In the second example, the adverb of manner quickly is placed between the verb leafed and the preposition through of the phrasal verb to leaf through.

Stress in Spoken English

When a verb followed by a preposition occurs at the end of a clause, it is usually the verb which is stressed in spoken English. In the following examples, the words which are stressed are printed in bold type.

e.g. No one likes to be laughed at.

— I need someone to confide in.

In the first example, the verb laughed followed by the preposition at occurs at the end of a clause, and the verb laughed is stressed. In the second example, the verb confide followed by the preposition in occurs at the end of a clause, and the verb confide is stressed.

It should be noted that, when used in a phrasal verb at the end of a clause, the prepositions after, into and over are often pronounced with somewhat greater emphasis than the verb. In this case, both the verb and the preposition are stressed. For example:

The twins are easy to look after.

The building would be difficult to break into.

You'll never guess whom I ran into.

I heard that someone was run over.

The prepositions above, across and through are also occasionally emphasized in this way. For example:

> The research papers were difficult to wade through.

Verb has an Object

In the case of some phrasal verbs consisting of a verb followed by a preposition, the verb and the preposition may each have an object. In the following examples, the objects are underlined.

e.g. I can make nothing of the situation.

— We talked my sister into agreeing.

In the first example, the verb make of the phrasal verb to make of has the object nothing, and the preposition of has the object situation. In the second example, the verb talked of the phrasal verb to talk into has the object sister, and the preposition into has the object agreeing.

The following are examples of phrasal verbs consisting of a verb followed by a preposition, where the verb may have an object. The objects of the verbs are underlined.

Each phrasal verb is followed by its meaning and an example of its use. The last example illustrates the use of the Passive Voice.

Verbs followed by Objects followed by Prepositions

drag into: involve unwillingly	Don't drag me into this discussion!
draw into: involve gradually	We managed to draw her into the conversation.
drum into: teach by repetition	We drummed the safety rules into the children.
frighten into: control by fear	The little girl frightened her brother into obeying her.
hold against: blame for	Please don't hold my mistakes against me.
lay before: present to	We will lay the evidence before the court.
let into: allow to share	Shall we let her into the secret?
make of: understand	Can you make anything of this message?
read into: find other meanings	You are reading too much into her remarks.
set against: make antagonistic	She likes to set people against one another.
set on: order to attack	We will set our dogs on any intruders.
talk into: persuade	Can you talk him into changing his mind?
thrust upon: force upon	We thrust the responsibility upon the treasurer.
write into: add to in writing	The terms were written into the lease.

VERB FOLLOWED BY AN ADVERB

Many phrasal verbs consist of a verb followed by an adverb. Some of these phrasal verbs are intransitive and some are transitive.

For instance, the intransitive phrasal verb to show up is formed from the verb to show followed by the adverb up. In the following example, the phrasal verb does not have an object.

At ten o'clock, her brother showed up.

The following are examples of intransitive phrasal verbs which consist of a verb followed by an adverb. Each phrasal verb is followed by its meaning and an example of its use.

Intransitive Verbs followed by Adverbs

blow over: pass	I wonder when the trouble will blow over.
boil away: disappear by boiling	If the water boils away, the stew will burn.
boil over: overflow by boiling	The soup boiled over.
bounce back: recover	He bounced back from his previous defeat.
buckle down: work seriously	You may fail your courses if you don't buckle down to work.
catch on: be widely accepted	Do you think the idea will catch on?
cloud over: become overcast	Although it clouded over in the afternoon, the rain held off.
die down: become less	After a few days, the excitement died down.
double up: bend over	We were doubled up with laughter.

drop in: visit	Please drop in any time.
fade away: become less	The sound gradually faded away.
fall off: become less	Attendance at the concerts has fallen off.
get away: escape	I hooked a fish, but it got away.
get by: barely succeed	She studied just hard enough to get by.
give in: admit defeat	I will never give in!
go on: continue	Please go on. Don't let me interrupt you.
grow up: become an adult	What do you want to do when you grow up?
keep on: persist in	He kept on changing the subject.
level off: stop rising	Prices finally levelled off.
log on: contact a computer	Do you know how to log on?
nod off: go to sleep	Half the bus passengers nodded off.
pass out: faint	It was so hot, I almost passed out.
pitch in: help	If everyone pitches in, the work will be done in a few minutes.
play along: pretend to agree	Let's play along until we find out what his plans are.
pull in: arrive (of vehicles)	The bus pulled in next to the curb.
pull out: leave (of vehicles)	The train pulled out at ten o'clock.
set off: leave	They set off at six o'clock in the morning.
settle down: become peaceful	After the excitement, the students found it difficult to settle down.
settle in: become used to	How are you settling in to your new job?
show up: arrive	She showed up at noon.

stay up: not go to bed	We stayed up until midnight.
step down: resign	He stepped down for health reasons.
step in: intervene	The government had to step in to save the business.
take off: leave the ground	The plane took off on time.
touch down: land (of planes)	The plane touched down.
watch out: beware	Watch out! The roads are icy.
wear off: gradually disappear	The feeling of excitement gradually wore off.

The transitive phrasal verb to sort out is formed from the verb to sort followed by the adverb out. For example:

We sorted out the papers.

In this example, the phrasal verb sorted out has the object papers.

The following are examples of transitive phrasal verbs which consist of a verb followed by an adverb. Each phrasal verb is followed by its meaning and an example of its use.

Transitive Verbs followed by Adverbs

back up: support	I will back up your story.
bail out: rescue	If you run into difficulties, who will bail you out?
breathe in: inhale	We breathed in the fresh air.
breathe out: exhale	I breathed out a sigh of relief.
bring back: return	She brought back her library books.
bring around: persuade	We gradually brought her around to our point of view.

bring up: raise	Bringing up children is never easy.
butter up: flatter	We buttered him up, hoping that he would agree to our proposal.
call in: ask to assist	I think it is time we called in an expert.
call off: cancel	We called off the meeting.
call up: telephone	Why don't you call him up?
cheer on: cheer, encourage	I will be there to cheer you on.
chop down: fell	They chopped down the dead tree.
clean up: tidy	The mayor asked everyone to help clean up the city streets.
fend off: repel	The goalie fended off every attack.
ferret out: find with difficulty	We managed to ferret out the information.
figure out: solve, understand	I can't figure out what happened.
fill in: complete	Please fill in this form.
fill out: complete	I filled out the form.
fill up: make full	We filled up the glasses with water.
give back: return	I gave back the bicycle I had borrowed.
give off: send out	Skunk cabbage gives off an unpleasant odor.
hand on:give to another person	I am not sorry to hand the responsibility on to you.
hand over: transfer	We had to hand the evidence over to the police.
hold back: restrain, delay	He is so enthusiastic, it is hard to hold him back.
iron out: remove	I am sure we can iron out every difficulty.
knock out: make unconscious	Boxers are often knocked out.

lap up: accept eagerly	The public lapped up the story.
lay off: put out of work	The company laid off seventy workers.
leave behind: leave, not bring	I accidentally left my umbrella behind.
leave out: omit	Tell me what happened. Don't leave anything out!
let down: disappoint	We will let him down if we don't arrive on time.
look up: find (information)	We looked up the word in a dictionary.
make up: invent	She likes to make up stories.
pass up: not take advantage	I couldn't pass up such an opportunity.
phase in: introduce gradually	The new programme will be phased in over the next six months.
phase out: cease gradually	The practice will gradually be phased out.
pick up: collect	You may pick up the papers at the office.
pin down: get a commitment	When the guest speaker is pinned down, we can set a date for the conference.
play down: de-emphasize	He played down the importance of the news.
point out: draw attention to	She pointed out the advantages of the proposal.
polish off: finish	We polished off the rest of the apple pie.
pull down: demolish	Many old buildings are pulled down to make way for new ones.
pull off: succeed	Do you think she can pull off her plan?
put away: put in proper place	It is time to put the toys away.

put off: postpone	We cannot put off the meeting again.
reel off: recite a long list	She reeled off a long list of names.
rope in: persuade to help	We roped in everyone we could to help with the work.
rub out: erase	Be sure to rub out all the pencil marks.
scale down: reduce	Because of lack of funds, we had to scale down our plans.
sell off: dispose of by selling	We sold off all the books and furniture.
set back: delay	This could set back the project by several years.
single out: select from others	You have been singled out for special attention.
size up: assess	I quickly sized up the situation.
sort out: organise	It will take some time to sort out this mess.
stammer out: stammer	They stammered out their apologies.
sum up: summarise	He summed up the discussion in a few well-chosen words.
summon up: gather	I attempted to summon up my courage.
take in: absorb	We tried to take in the new information.
take out: invite to a restaurant	May I take you out for supper?
take over: assume control	They will take over at the beginning of June.
talk over: discuss	Let us talk it over before we decide.
tear up: destroy by tearing	She tore up the letter.
think over: consider	I need some time to think it over.
think up: invent	What will they think up next?

track down:search for and find	We finally tracked him down at the bookstore.
trade in: give as part payment	Why don't you trade in your old vacuum cleaner for a new one?
try out: test by using	Would you like to try out my fountain pen?
turn away: refuse admission	The event was so popular that many people had to be turned away.
turn back: reverse direction	Every fall the clocks must be turned back by one hour.
water down: dilute	The soup has been watered down.
write down: make a note	I wrote down the instructions.
write off: cancel, regard as	They were forced to write off several irretrievable debts.
write up: compose in writing	I used my notes to write up the report.

Object of the Verb

In the case of transitive phrasal verbs consisting of a verb followed by an adverb, if the object of the verb is a noun, the object can usually either follow or precede the adverb. In the following examples, the objects are underlined.

e.g. I called off the meeting.

— I called the meeting off.

In the first example the object meeting follows the adverb off, while in the second example the object meeting precedes the adverb off. However, in the case of a few phrasal verbs, a noun object must usually follow the adverb.

e.g. We attempted to smooth over the disagreement.

In this example, the phrasal verb to smooth over is followed by the noun object disagreement. In this case, the object disagreement cannot be placed before the adverb over.

The following are examples of transitive phrasal verbs where a noun object must usually follow the adverb. Each phrasal verb is accompanied by its meaning and an example of its use. The objects of the verbs are underlined.

Verbs followed by Adverbs followed by Noun Objects

drum up: raise	She has drummed up support for the plan.
paper over: repair superficially	They attempted to paper over their differences.
smooth over: improve	We tried to smooth over the situation.

In the case of transitive phrasal verbs consisting of a verb followed by an adverb, if the object of the verb is a pronoun, the object must usually precede the adverb. In the following examples, the pronoun objects are underlined.

e.g. I called it off.

– We attempted to smooth it over.

In these examples, the pronoun object it precedes the adverbs off and over. Most transitive phrasal verbs may be used in the Passive Voice.

e.g. The meeting was called off by me.

– The disagreement was smoothed over.

In these examples, the phrasal verbs to call off and to smooth over are used in the Passive Voice.

Adverb of Manner Modifying the Verb

In the case of a phrasal verb consisting of a verb followed by an adverb, the verb and the adverb usually may not be separated by an adverb of manner. In the following example, the adverb of manner is underlined.

e.g. I hurriedly called off the meeting.

In this example, the adverb of manner hurriedly precedes the phrasal verb called off. The adverb hurriedly may also be placed at the beginning or the end of the sentence, but may not be placed between the verb called and the adverb off.

Stress in Spoken English

When a phrasal verb consisting of a verb followed by an adverb occurs at the end of a clause, it is usually the adverb which is stressed in spoken English. In the following examples, the words which are stressed are printed ion bold type.

e.g. How did that come about?

Please drop in whenever you have time.

In the first example, the verb come followed by the adverb about occurs at the end of a clause, and the adverb about is stressed. In the second example, the verb drop followed by the adverb in occurs at the end of a clause, and the adverb in is stressed.

Ergative Verbs

It should be noted that there are a few phrasal verbs consisting of a verb followed by an adverb, which have the same meaning whether they are used transitively or intransitively. For example:

The engineer slowed down the train.

The train slowed down.

In the first example, the phrasal verb to slow down is used transitively, with the object train. In the second example, the phrasal verb to slow down is used intransitively, without naming the originator of the action. In these two examples, it can be seen that the object of the transitive verb is the subject of the intransitive verb. However, the general meaning of the two sentences is the same. Verbs which can be used in this way may be referred to as ergative verbs.

The following are examples of expressions which can function as ergative phrasal verbs. Each ergative phrasal verb is followed by its meaning and examples of its use.

Ergative Phrasal Verbs

blare out: make a loud sound	The loudspeakers blared out the music.
	The music blared out.
	The bridge blew up.
break up: break into pieces	The icebreaker broke up the ice.
	The ice broke up.
burn down: destroy by fire	We burned down the old barn.
	The old barn burned down.

calm down: become calm	I calmed down the child.
	The child calmed down.
dry out: become dry	The sun dried out the earth.
	The earth dried out.
get across: transmit	We got our point across to the audience.
	Our point got across to the audience.
liven up: become lively	He livened up the party.
	The party livened up.
pull through:recover from,	The doctor pulled her through the illness.
	She pulled through the illness.
roll up: wrap into a cylinder	I rolled up the window blind.
	The window blind rolled up.
shut down: close, stop working	They shut down the factory.
	The factory shut down.
wake up: stop sleeping	I woke her up.
	She woke up.
wash out: remove by washing	We washed out the dye.
	The dye washed out.
wear away: gradually remove	Water wore away the rock.
	The rock wore away.

VERBS FOLLOWED BY PREPOSITIONS AND VERBS FOLLOWED BY ADVERBS

It has been seen that the position of pronoun objects, adverbs of manner and stress in spoken English varies according to whether a verb is followed by a preposition or by an adverb.

These differences are summarised in the following table. The verbs to sit and to turn are used as examples. The verb to sit is followed by on used as a preposition, whereas the verb to turn is followed by on used as an adverb.

Verb followed by Preposition	*Verb followed by Adverb*
Pronoun object is placed after the preposition:	Pronoun object is placed before the adverb:
I sat on it.	I turned it on.
Adverb of manner may be placed between verb and preposition:	Adverb of manner may not be placed between verb and adverb:
I sat quietly on it.	I quietly turned it on.
Verb is stressed:	Adverb is stressed:
This is what I sat on.	This is what I turned on.

Because of the differences summarised above, it is important to be able to distinguish between a verb followed by a preposition, and a verb followed by an adverb.

Adverb Phrases of Location and Phrasal Verbs Followed by Objects

In many cases, it is necessary to distinguish between an ordinary verb followed by an adverb phrase of location, and a phrasal verb followed by an object.

e.g. I turned up the street.

— I turned up the volume.

In the first example, the verb turned is followed by the adverb phrase of location up the street. In the second example, the phrasal verb turned up is followed by the object volume. In this example, the phrasal verb turned up has the meaning increased.

In the first example, street is the object of the preposition up. If the object is changed to a pronoun, the pronoun must follow the preposition:

— I turned up the street.

— I turned up it.

In the second example, volume is the object of the phrasal verb turned up. If the object is changed to a pronoun, the pronoun must precede the adverb up.

— I turned up the volume.

— I turned it up.

In the first example, if the verb is modified by an adverb of manner, the adverb of manner may precede the adverb phrase of location:

— I turned up the street.

— I turned quickly up the street.

In the second example, if the verb is modified by an adverb of manner, the adverb of manner may not be placed between the two parts of the phrasal verb:

— I turned up the volume.

— I quickly turned up the volume.

Words used as Prepositions

It is also necessary to be able to distinguish between a phrasal verb consisting of a verb followed by a preposition, and a phrasal verb consisting of a transitive verb followed by an adverb. In many cases it is possible to make the distinction by means of the preposition or adverb following the verb.

For example, the following words are used in phrasal verbs as prepositions, but are not usually used in phrasal verbs as adverbs following transitive verbs:

after	against
at	before
by	for
from	into
of	to
toward	with
without	

In contrast, the following words are used in phrasal verbs as adverbs following transitive verbs, but are not usually used in phrasal verbs as prepositions:

along	aside
away	back
behind	down
forward	out
together	up

It should be noted that of these words, aside, away, back, forward, out and together are usually never used as prepositions. In contrast, the words along, behind, down and up are often used as prepositions, but are not usually used as prepositions in phrasal verbs.

The following words present more difficulty, since they can be used in phrasal verbs both as prepositions and as adverbs following transitive verbs:

across	around or round
in	off

on or upon	over
through	

Thus, it is advisable to study which phrasal verbs use these words as prepositions, and which phrasal verbs use these words as adverbs. The following table gives examples of phrasal verbs containing each of these words.

The left-hand column gives phrasal verbs consisting of verbs followed by prepositions, while the right-hand column gives phrasal verbs consisting of transitive verbs followed by adverbs.

Words used as Prepositions or Adverbs

Verb + Preposition	*Transitive Verb + Adverb*
come across	get across (an idea)
cut across	put across (an idea)
run across	
stumble across	
Verb + Preposition	*Transitive Verb + Adverb*
hang around	bring round
lounge around	
mill around	
pass around	
rally round	
show around	
Verb + Preposition	*Transitive Verb + Adverb*
confide in	break in
deal in	breathe in

join in
fill in
hand in
phase in
rope in
take in
trade in

call in

Verb + Preposition	*Transitive Verb + Adverb*
glance off	call off
keep off	fend off
warn off	give off
	lay off
	pair off
	pension off
	polish off
	pull off
	put off
	reel off
	sell off
	shrug off
	turn off
	write off

Verb + Preposition	*Transitive Verb + Adverb*
bank on	cheer on
border on	hand on
build on	try on

call on
come upon
count on
dawn on
decide on
dwell on
enlarge on
expand on
frown on
grow on
hinge on
live on
pick on
prey on
reckon on
survive on
thrust upon
touch on
verge on

turn on

Verb + Preposition

get over
go over
run over
watch over
smooth over

Transitive Verb + Adverb

take over
talk over
think over
paper over

Verb + Preposition	*Transitive Verb + Adverb*
break through	pull through
get through	
go through	
leaf through	
look through	
sail through	
scrape through	
see through	
sit through	
wade through	

PHRASAL VERBS CAN BE USED AS EITHER PREPOSITION OR ADVERB

Some phrasal verbs consist of an intransitive verb followed by a word which may function either as an adverb or as a preposition. For example:

– We passed by.

– We passed by the library.

In the first example, the word by of the phrasal verb passed by functions as an adverb. In the second example, the word by of the phrasal verb passed by functions as a preposition which has the object library.

The following are examples of phrasal verbs which contain words which may function either as adverbs or as prepositions. Each phrasal verb is followed by its meaning and examples of its use. The objects of the prepositions are underlined.

Intransitive Verbs followed by words which may function either as Adverbs or Prepositions

break through: appear	The sun broke through.
	The sun broke through the clouds.
do without: survive without	We had to do without.
	We had to do without electricity.
glance off: hit and bounce off	The ball glanced off.
	The ball glanced off the wall.
go without: not have	They went without.
	They went without food.
hang around: stay near	We hung around.
	We hung around the movie theater.
join in: become involved in	I joined in.
	I joined in the game.
lounge around: relax in	We lounged around.
	We lounged around the living room.
pass by: pass	I passed by.
	I passed by the house.
	We rallied round our class president.
sail through: succeed easily	She sailed through.
	She sailed through the exam.
scrape through:barely succeed	They scraped through.
	They scraped through the course.
turn off: leave a road	We turned off.
	We turned off the main highway.

Verb has an Object

There are a few phrasal verbs consisting of a verb followed by a word which may function either as an adverb or as a preposition, where the verb may have an object. In the following examples the objects are underlined.

e.g. We passed the candies around.

— We passed the candies around the class.

In each of these examples, the verb passed of the phrasal verb to pass around has the object candies. In the first example, the word around functions as an adverb, while in the second example, the word around functions as a preposition with the object class.

The following are examples of phrasal verbs consisting of a verb followed by a word which may function either as an adverb or as a preposition, where the verb may have an object.

Each phrasal verb is followed by its meaning and examples of its use. The objects of the verbs and prepositions are underlined. The last example illustrates the use of the Passive Voice.

Verbs followed by objects followed by words which may function either as Adverbs or Prepositions

cross off: put a line through	I crossed his name off. I crossed his name off the list.
pass around: distribute	I passed the papers around. I passed the papers around the class.
warn off: warn to leave	We were warned off.

	We were warned off the premises.

VERB FOLLOWED BY AN ADVERB FOLLOWED BY A PREPOSITION

There are several commonly used phrasal verbs which consist of a verb, followed by an adverb, followed by a preposition. For example:

I went along with the idea.

In this example, the phrasal verb went along with consists of the verb to go, followed by the adverb along, followed by the preposition with which has the object idea.

The following table gives examples of phrasal verbs which consist of a verb, followed by an adverb, followed by a preposition. Each phrasal verb is followed by its meaning and an example of its use.

Verbs followed by Adverbs followed by Prepositions

add up to: amount to	It is hard to see what that adds up to.
back down from: withdraw, avoid	She never backs down from a challenge.
back out of: not fulfill	I wish I could back out of the agreement.
boil down to: can be reduced to	All his arguments boil down to a belief in the supernatural.
bow out of: withdraw	He bowed out of the race.
brush up on: refresh knowledge of	I must brush up on my English.
carry on with: continue with	We carried on with our conversation.

catch up to: overtake	The boy ran quickly to catch up with his friends.
clean up after: tidy for	She spent half her time cleaning up after the children.
come down to: can be reduced to	Your choices come down to these.
come down with: become ill with	She came down with a cold.
come out in: develop	He came out in a rash.
come up against: meet an obstacle	They came up against many difficulties.
come up with: produce	She came up with a solution to the problem.
creep up on: approach undetected	Old age tends to creep up on one.
cry out for: urgently require	The education system is crying out for improvement.
cut back on: reduce	The government has cut back on spending.
do away with: abolish	We want to do away with delays.
face up to: accept and deal with	It is best to face up to one's problems.
fall back on: turn to for help	Because of unexpected expenses, we had to fall back on our savings.
fit in with: be suited to	You don't fit in with this group.
get away with: not be punished	He got away with being late for school.
get in on: manage to participate in	I want to get in on the planning for the new school.
give up on: stop trying	I've given up on the situation.
go along with: agree, not resist	I'm willing to go along with your idea.
go back on: break a promise	He never goes back on his word.

go through with: fulfill, carry out	Are you going to go through with your plan to conduct a survey?
grow out of: become too big for	My son has grown out of most of his clothes.
hold out for: not compromise	We want to hold out for better conditions.
lead up to: be a preparation for	The first thirty chapters of the book lead up to the dramatic conclusion.
live up to: maintain a standard	She has lived up to her reputation as a great singer.
log on to: contact a computer	She logged on to the new system.
look down on: regard as inferior	He looks down on his classmates.
look forward to: anticipate	I'm looking forward to the holidays.
look out for: watch for	Look out for fallen branches.
look up to: admire	We looked up to her.
make up for: compensate for	She tried to make up for her past mistakes.
pull out of: leave (of vehicles)	The train pulled out of the station.
push on with: go ahead, continue	I must push on with my work.
put up with: endure, tolerate	Bus passengers must often put up with crowded conditions.
read up on: read about	Whenever I travel, I like to read up on the place I am going to visit.
rub off on: acquire from someone	Some of his enthusiasm has rubbed off on me.
run up against: meet	One runs up against many different kinds of people.

send away for: order by mail	We sent away for warm winter boots.
stick up for: defend, support	Will you stick up for me?
stock up on: lay in supplies	We should stock up on bananas.
talk down to: speak patronizingly	He always talks down to people younger than he is.
walk away with: win easily	They walked away with all the prizes.
watch out for: beware of	Watch out for snakes.
wriggle out of: avoid	She always tries to wriggle out of her responsibilities.
zero in on: focus on	Let us zero in on the heart of the problem.

Verb has an Object

There are a few phrasal verbs consisting of a verb, followed by an adverb, followed by a preposition, where the verb may have an object. In the following example, the objects are underlined.

e.g. We played them off against each other.

In this example, the verb played of the phrasal verb to play off against has the object them, while the preposition against has the object each other.

The following are examples of phrasal verbs consisting of a verb, followed by an adverb, followed by a preposition, where the verb may have an object.

Each phrasal verb is followed by its meaning and an example of its use. The objects of the phrasal verbs are underlined.

Verbs followed by Objects followed by Adverbs followed by Prepositions

get over with: undergo, finish	If I must visit the dentist, I prefer to get it over with as soon as possible.
let in on: allow to share	We let them in on the secret.
put down to: attribute to	We put his bad temper down to fatigue.
put up to: urge to do wrong	She put me up to playing a trick on the teacher.
take out on:vent bad feelings on	She took her dissatisfaction with her job out on her neighbors.
take up on: accept an offer	I would like to take you up on your offer.
talk out of: dissuade from	We tried to talk him out of retiring.

7

Verbs that Take Prepositions

Phrasal verbs, also known as two-word verbs, are verbs that require specific prepositions. Because preposition following the verb affects the verb's meaning, writers must use the proper verb-preposition combination in order to communicate clearly. Saying "Jane believed John" means something entirely different than saying "Jane believed in John."

Using the wrong preposition leads to confusing or awkward prose. Saying "Jane believed to John," for example, does not make sense. Below are only some of the most common verbs that take prepositions. The UWC has excellent resources for a more comprehensive list of verbs that take prepositions.

account for:	Nothing could account for his depression.
accuse... of:	They accused him of robbing a bank.
agree on:	No one could agree on anything.
agree with:	I agree with the man who is speaking.

allude to: It is not polite to allude to someone's disability.

apologise for: He did apologise for running away.

apologise to: The leader did not want to apologise to the people.

apply for: Every June college graduates apply for jobs.

approve of: We do not approve of his behaviour.

argue with: It does little good to argue with a judge.

argue about: A judge does not want you to argue about anything unless you have a good case.

arrive at: He arrived at a conclusion quickly.

ask for: Children like to ask their parents for gifts, but they especially like to ask for special toys.

become of: John has disappeared; I do not know what has become of him.

believe in: Do you believe in magic?

belong to: Whom does this pet belong to? It belongs to her.

blame... for: Don't blame me for your problems!

blame... on: Don't blame your problems on me!

borrow from: He has borrowed enough money from the bank.

care for: She enjoys the time she can care for her nieces and nephews.

come from: She came from Honduras with her family.

compare with: How does a small car compare with a large car?

complain about: He is always complaining about something.

compliment on: Compliment them on their performance.

congratulate on: They deserve to be congratulated on (or for) their good work.

consent to: The parents refused to consent to their son's marriage.

consist of: The solution consists of some strange chemicals.

convince of: I am convinced of his good intentions.

decide between: I cannot decide between the two.

delight in: My child delights in watching the ducks.

depend on/upon: Do not depend upon other people.

detract from: Such behavior detracts from your beauty.

dream about/of: We are dreaming about going to Paris.

excuse... for: The teacher excused the child for his behavior.

explain... to: It is difficult to explain a problem to people who don't care.

happen to: Oh, I just happened to be in the neighbourhood.

hear of:	Have you ever heard of something like that?
hear aboutL:	Did you hear about Mary? She's got a new job.
hear from:	Did you get a letter from him? I never hear from him.
insist on:	The decorator insists on blue drapes.
invite... to:	It would be a good idea to invite him to the party.
laugh about:	We laugh about the crazy things we used to do.
laugh at:	It's not nice to laugh at someone.
laugh with:	When a person laughs, it's good to laugh with him.
listen for:	I'm listening for the mail carrier; she should be here by now.
listen to:	Listen to me when I'm speaking to you.
look at:	It is not polite to look at someone for a long time.
look for:	My child is lost! We must look for him.
object to:	Most people do not object to helping someone in need.
prefer... to:	I prefer red cars to blue cars
plan on:	Why don't you plan on staying at our place?
provide... with:	My parents have provided me with enough money to last for one month.

recover from: It often takes a long time to recover from a serious illness.

refer to: If you are referring to me, you should say so.

rely on: I can always rely on my strength.

remind... of: you remind me of a bear.

search for: We searched for the lost child for three hours, but we couldn't find her.

spend... on: Anna spent all of her money on a new car.

substitute for: When I was absent, William substituted for me.

talk to: When I am talking to you, I expect you to listen to me.

talk about: It is not nice to talk about people when they are not present.

thank... for: Thank you for the nice gift.

vote for: You should vote for my candidate.

wait for: Please wait for me! I'll be ready in a moment.

wait on: No, I will not bring you breakfast in bed. I won't wait on you like that.

work for: We should all work for the good of mankind. Mukesh works for that big company.

worry about: Mothers always worry about their children, and so do fathers.

wrestle with: We spent three hours wrestling with that problem, but we could not solve it.

8

Use of "To" and "Through"

The situated interpretation of spatial particles, such as English prepositions, does not solely derive from the preposition itself. Rather, other form-classes which collocate with the preposition bear on the interpretation of the preposition in context. For instance, consider the following noun phrases:

(1) The fruit in the bowl

(2) The crack in the bowl

What these examples illustrate is that a particular Trajector (TR) can, in conjunction with a particular Landmark (LM), affect the interpretation of a preposition. On one hand, the interpretation ascribed to the sentence in (1) is that the LM, the bowl, contains or surrounds the TR, the fruit. On the other hand, in (2) the conventional interpretation is that the TR, the crack, constitutes a flaw which is part of the bowl.

Additionally, the crack may either appear as part of the interior or exterior of the bowl. Language users do not normally derive an interpretation for (2), in which an entity identified as the crack is somehow located within the confines of the bowl, i.e.

the interior space bounded by the bowl, in the same way that entities such as fruit can be. Clearly, our interpretation of the conceptual spatial relation denoted by a preposition, such as in, is in part constrained by sentential context, that is, by the characteristics of the actions or entities which are designated.

A crack is a different kind of entity from fruit. In conceptual terms, a crack is inherently relational, requiring a LM of which it constitutes a subpart, while fruit is a conceptually distinct entity. The different status of these two items differentially affects the exact interpretation of the relationship designated by the preposition.

In this way, the meaning assigned to the preposition is "distributed" across the sentence. Since Brugman and Lakoff's work on the English preposition over, it has been common in cognitive semantics to assume that the nature of spatial meaning is due to the contribution of distinct senses associated with a preposition, rather than allowing sentential context a significant role. For instance, consider the following in sentences:

(3) Sam climbed over the wall

(4) The bird flew over the wall

(5) Sam walked over the hill

Lakoff analysed these sentences as representing three distinct senses for over, i.e. as reflecting three distinct schematisations. These schematisations involve presence or absence of contact between the TR and LM, as in (3) and (5), or presence (as in (5)) or 2 absence (as in (3) and (4)) of horizontal extension. This highly granular approach to lexical polysemy has been criticised for a number of reasons.

Sinha and Kuteva observe that such "full specification" approaches to spatial particles derive from the implicit assumption that "spatial relational meaning [...] is carried by the locative particle, and only by the locative particle".

That is, Lakoff and those following his analysis of over have failed to recognise that in examples such as these, the TR and/or LM are crucially contributing to the trajectory shape, while the verb contributes path information. These arguments suggest that it may be erroneous to represent the preposition itself as conventionally contributing meaning at the level of specificity that has sometimes been claimed.

Of course, to suggest that the spatial meaning associated with prepositions is distributed over the utterance in which the form occurs does not entail that the preposition itself is devoid of meaning. On the contrary, prepositions do have conventional meanings associated with them, including a functional element.

However, the precise interpretation assigned to the prepositions is constrained and delimited by the sentential context, including the TR.NP, LM.NP, and verb which occur in the utterance. Nowhere is this clearer than with the so-called "prepositions of movement", which present an excellent "laboratory" for studying what prepositions do conventionally provide in terms of information about a spatial scene (a conceptualised relation between a TR and a LM, e.g., The cat is on the mat), complex conceptualisations, and how the interpretation associated with a preposition is constrained and nuanced by other elements in the sentence.

In specific terms, we argue against the widespread assumption that many so called "dynamic" prepositions denote motion. In particular, such analyses have conflicted the distinct concepts of motion, orientation, goal, trajectory and path.

Information relating to motion and trajectory is derived from sentential context, typically from verbs, but in some cases general pragmatics and our knowledge of the world. In order to illustrate this, we provide an analysis of to and through, suggesting that while to codes for orientation and goal, but not path and motion, through codes for path, but not goal, orientation, and motion.

CASE OF OVER

As the English preposition over has been so extensively studied, it provides a useful point of departure for the perspective we will advance. It has often been suggested that certain prepositions encode "movement". For instance, Lakoff following Brugman argued that the central spatial sense associated with over constitutes a 'dynamic' above-across meaning element. Lakoff explicitly claims that this sense encodes a "path", along which the TR travels. Evidence for this analysis comes from examples such as (6).

(6) a. The cat jumped over the wall

b. The UFO flew over the city

A central issued raised by the claim that over has a "movement" above-across sense associated with it is whether any preposition encodes motion with accompanying trajectory information. We argue that they do not.

Rather, a motion reading follows from the nature of the activity being engaged in, the nature of the TR, and/or the nature of the LM. That is, the complex conceptualisation which arises is due to integration of sentential elements as interpreted through our knowledge of the world. Hence, the information which results in a "dynamic" reading is distributed across the sentence, rather than being solely due to the preposition.

Two additional issues arise from this analysis. First, in conducting semantic analyses of prepositions we need to carefully identify which meaning components are conventionalised by a particular preposition.

In 4 we introduce the notion of a conventional functional element, which we suggest arises due to the spatio-geometric character of the central spatial sense associated with a particular preposition. Path, is a functional element which is conventionally associated with a number of prepositions (although over is not one of them).

By identifying the conventional spatiogeometric semantics and functional element(s) associated with a particular preposition, we demonstrate how it is possible to avoid attributing a particular meaning to a preposition which properly arises from its interaction with other sentential elements.

The second issue relates to the concept of "movement". It appears that cognitive semanticists have often tacitly conflicted the notions of trajectory, path and motion, in a hybrid category of "movement" or "dynamism".

An important aspect of our argument is that motion, trajectory and path (as well as orientation and goal) are distinct (albeit related and often correlated) concepts.

Motion involves change of an entity's location over time; 2) The trajectory is the shape of the motion event; and 3) Path is a consequence of an end-point or goal being related (i.e., connected) to a starting-point or locational source by virtue of a series of contiguous points.

In order to begin to address the two issues described in the foregoing, let's consider the sentence in (6) a. The case for attributing a dynamic above-across sense to over in examples such as (6) a. relies on implied reasoning which runs as follows:

(1) a spatial scene is conceptualised in which a cat starts from a position on one side of the wall and comes to be in a position on the other side;

(2) there is nothing in the sentence, 4 other than the preposition over, which indicates the trajectory followed by the cat;

(3) and as a trajectory is entailed by a moving entity, therefore, over must prompt for an above and-across trajectory.

But this conclusion is a non sequitur. Simply because the trajectory is not explicitly denoted by specific linguistic forms (formal expression) does not entail that such information is otherwise absent from the interpretation (and hence attributable to over). On this view, all elements that are salient in the interpretation of a scene must be coded linguistically.

Rather than representing the "spatial" meaning of prepositions as carrying detailed information about each scene being described, including whether or not there is a trajectory and therefore the information that the TR is capable of undergoing motion, we argue that they prompt for schematic conceptualisations-in previous work we have termed this a proto-scene-that are interpreted within the particular contexts in which they occur.

Under our analysis, motion (and the trajectory which an entity in motion entails) is prompted for by the verb, and what we know about cats, their goals, walls (as impenetrable barriers to forward motion) and the key spatial configuration (including the resultant functional element) denoted by the preposition.

In (6) a, the verb jumped does prompt for a conceptualisation involving motion, which entails the TR following a trajectory. The interpretation of the above-across movement in (6) a. is not prompted for by over (i.e. the concept of the TR in motion is not a semantic attribute of the proto-scene, nor for any of the other distinct senses associated with over), but rather arises from the integration of linguistic prompts at the conceptual level.

Most of the information required to integrate the linguistic prompts and construct a mental conceptualisation of the spatial scene is filled in by inferencing and real-world knowledge.

In turn, this knowledge constrains the possible interpretations that over can have in this particular sentence. In the interpretation of (6) a, such encyclopedic knowledge includes (at the very least):

(1) our understanding of the action of jumping, and in particular our knowledge of the kind of jumping cats are likely to engage in (that is, not straight up in the air as on a trampoline and not from a bungee cord suspended from a tree branch extending above the wall);

(2) our knowledge of cats (for instance, that they cannot physically hover in the air the way a hummingbird can);

(3) our knowledge of the nature of walls (that they

provide vertical, impenetrable obstacles to forward motion); and

(4) our knowledge of force dynamics such as gravity (which tells us that a cat cannot remain in mid air indefinitely and that if the cat jumped from the ground such that, at some key point, its trajectory matches the relation described by over the wall, then it would have to come to rest beyond the wall, providing an arc trajectory.

Thus, we argue that the interpretation regarding the above-across trajectory in sentence (6) a. is not prompted for by over, but rather arises from the integration of linguistic prompts at the conceptual level, in a way that is maximally coherent with and contingent on our real-world interactions.

We further suggest that part of the general understanding of this particular sentence involves the interpretation of the wall as an obstacle which the cat is attempting to overcome. Hence, the salient spatial location is the point at which the cat jumped high enough to overcome the obstacle. To make this point more concrete, consider Figure 1, which offers an approximate depiction of the complex conceptualisation constructed in the interpretation of (6) a.

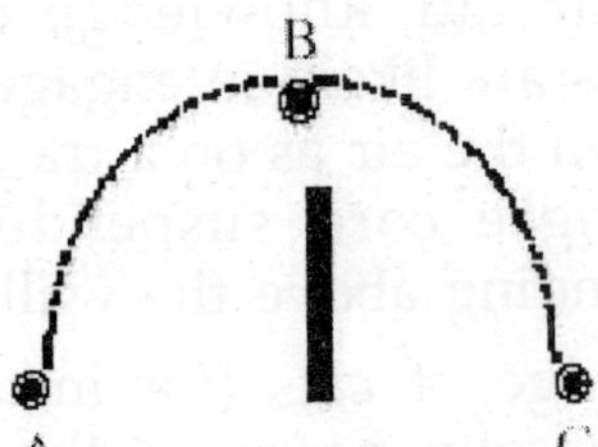

Figure 1 The cat jumped over the wall

In Figure 1 the various positions occupied by the TR, the cat, along its trajectory are represented by the three spheres labelled A, B, and C. Notice that only point B-the point at which the cat is higher than but in potential reach of the wall-is explicitly mentioned in the sentence. Points A and C are inferred from what we know about jumping, cats, and walls.

The verb jumped codes self-propelled motion using a solid surface to push off from, thus, point A is implied as the initial point of the trajectory. The prompts are integrated in such a way that the trajectory initiated by the verb jump intersects with point B.

Our knowledge of real-world force dynamics fills in position C. Put another way, if a cat begins at point A and passes through point B, then given our knowledge of gravity and the kind of jumping cats are able to do, point C is entailed.

Accordingly, the problem with attributing a dynamic sense to over, is that such an analysis fails to fully distinguish between formal expression in language, which represents certain limited information, and patterns of conceptualisation, which integrate "distributed" information prompted for by other linguistic elements of the sentence together with our knowledge of the world.

Over does not itself prompt for an above across sense, that is, for a trajectory, which is ipso facto entailed by motion.

Now let's consider the example in (6) b. As with our discussion of (6) a, we suggest a trajectory is prompted for by virtue of the lexeme flew, together with what we know about UFOs, and the kind of activities they engage in.

The shape of the trajectory is constrained both by over (which provides the information that the TR is higher than the LM) and the nature of the LM, the city, which is horizontally extended.

However, even though the interpretation of the trajectory is constrained, the information provided by the linguistic code nevertheless underdetermines the exact shape of the trajectory. Indeed, we find at least three plausible "construals" for this sentence, as illustrated below:

Construal 1 stipulates that the UFO flew above and across the city, such that it originated in a position not above the city, moved over the city, and came to be in a position beyond the city (Figure 2).

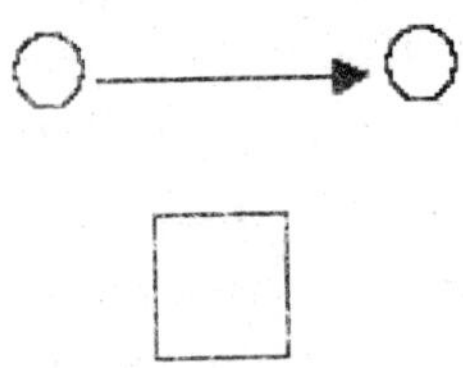

Figure 2. The UFO flew over the city (construal 1).

Construal 2 stipulates that the UFO moved from a position in which it was not over the city, to a position such that it came to be directly over the city (Figure 3).

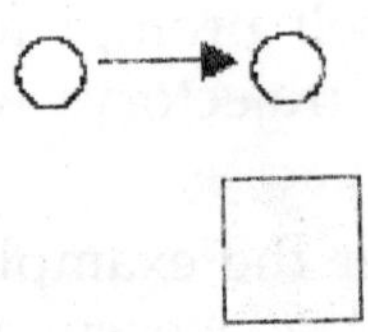

Figure 3. The UFO flew over the city (construal 2)

The third construal is one in which the UFO flies around while remaining above the city (Figure 4).

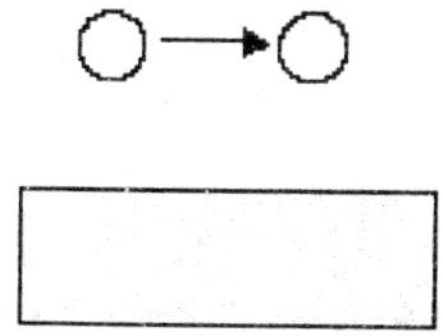

Figure 4. The UFO flew over the city (construal 3).

The fact that there are (at least) three distinct construals for this sentence illustrates that the TR.NP, LM.NP and verb of motion can be integrated in a number of ways. This, in turn, illustrates

1) the importance of integration and
2) that lexical items are merely prompts for a process of conceptual integration (rather than "fully-specified" entities).

In sum, we have argued that the conceptualisations in which over participates do often involve the notion of motion and, hence, a trajectory. However, the motion and accompanying trajectory interpretation is prompted for by the conventional meaning associated with other elements, notably the verb, but also the TR, as in the plane, or the LM, as LMs which serve as obstacles to forward motion or horizontally extended LMs such as cities.

These sentential elements serve to constrain and delimit how over is 7 interpreted, and in this sense, the spatial relation designated by over in any given local context is "distributed" across the sentence. A greater appreciation of the role of sentential context in meaning construction suggests then, that over does not have, and indeed no English preposition has, a "movement" sense associated with it.

Nevertheless, certain prepositions, such as over, do seem more likely to participate in "movement" readings than other prepositions, such as on. To understand how and why over often participates in "movement" readings, while on is less likely to do so, we require a descriptively adequate characterisation not just of the preposition's core spatio-geometric semantics (i.e., the precise nature of the TR-LM configuration), but also the functional elements (s) which arise as a consequence of these spatial properties.

But note that even a "non-dynamic" preposition, such as on, can participate in a movement reading, as in Chris ran on the highway for an hour. In 5 and 6 we consider two prepositions which have often been assumed to designate "movement", namely to and through.

By virtue of carefully teasing apart the distinct concepts orientation, trajectory, goal and path, contrasting these with motion, and providing an descriptively adequate characterisation of these two prepositions, we seek to demonstrate that it is erroneous to assume that such prepositions designate "dynamism" and a trajectory which is inevitably entailed by an entity in motion.

ATEMPORALITY AND MOTION

At base, the core semantics associated with prepositions has to do with spatial configurations. Moreover, the spatial configurations in question are relational, mediating a physical locator (the LM), and a physical locand (the TR). The nature of the relation profiled by prepositions can be distinguished from that profiled by another salient relational class, namely verbs.

Verbs profile processes which necessarily evolve over conceived time. While the temporal dimension is the essence of the profiled relation encoded by verbs, it is ignored by prepositions (in terms of their core spatial characterisation). Evidence that prepositions encode relations which are atemporal comes from the so-called reflexive senses.

Spatial reflexivity is the phenomenon whereby a single entity which occupies multiple positions is conceptualised such that two salient positions occupied by the entity are integrated into a TR-LM spatial configuration. A preposition such as over can be used to mediate a spatial relation between the two positions, even though the same entity cannot simultaneously occupy two distinct spatial positions in the world.

The dynamic character of experience is re-analysed as a static spatial configuration. Langacker discusses this gestalt-like static conceptualisation of a dynamic process as summary scanning. Consider (7).

(7) The fence fell over.

In (7), the TR, the fence, is distinguished in its initial (upright) position from its final position, in which it is lying horizontally on the ground. In our everyday experience with 8 the world, sometimes we see erect objects, such as a fence, fall through a ninety-degree arc to a resting position on the ground. We also frequently observe the same object at separate times in two different positions, i.e. at one point in time when the object is erect, at a later point in time when the object is resting on the ground; in this situation, we typically infer that the object has moved through a ninety-degree arc.

From these experiences, a conceptual spatial relation is abstracted (via both summary scanning and inferencing), mediating the two temporally situated locations into a single (atemporal) spatial configuration. In the world, no such spatial configuration exists; after all, the same fence cannot be in two locations at the same time. However, by conceptualising the fence reflexively, the same entity can be both the TR and the LM (Figure 5).

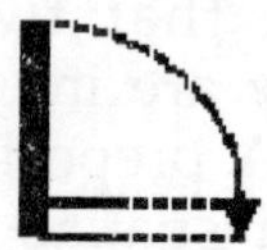

Figure 5. The reflexive sense

The consequence of the claim that spatial particles and prepositions do not profile temporally-evolving processes, but rather atemporal spatial configurations is that prepositions, ipso facto cannot encode motion. This follows as motion results from change of location over time, and hence constitutes a temporally-evolving process.

ORIENTATION, TRAJECTORY, PATH AND GOAL

The functional element (or elements) associated with a particular preposition arises as a consequence of our continued and ubiquitous interaction with spatial scenes involving certain spatial configurations. Take for instance a spatial scene involving a TR and a bounded LM-a landmark which can be characterised by the spatio-geometric property of having four sides, such as a box, and hence possessing an interior and exterior. One consequence of our interaction with certain kinds of bounded LMs is that we experience them in terms of containment. Containment itself is a complex relation, involving numerous functional consequences.

In the guise of containers, bounded LMs constrain and delimit movement of their TRs, as in a coffee cup which constrains the coffee it contains to a specific location, or a prison cell, which restricts the movements of a convict. In certain 9 circumstances, constraining movement can be understood as providing support, thus a cut flower can be held in an upright position as a result of being placed in a vase.

If the boundaries of the container are opaque, they prevent us from seeing beyond them, or the interior area from being seen by entities outside, as in a walled garden or a windowless room. Containers can also provide protection, as with a jeweller's safe. For the elements within a container, the container surrounds and largely determines the environment in which those entities exist. Different aspects of the experience of containment are profiled by the various uses of the spatial particles in and out.

A second consequence of our interaction with bounded LMs is that they can serve as goals. For instance, after leaving work, for many people the goal is to arrive at home in order to interact with family, relax, etc. The salient space in which these anticipated activities take place is a bounded LM, the living quarters; thus, being in the salient space, the bounded LM, is closely related to achieving goals.

A third way in which we interact with bounded LMs is that we emerge from them, as when we leave home each morning. Equally, we draw other entities from bounded LMs, as when a jeweller withdraws a diamond broach from a safe. In this way, bounded LMs have source properties, as lexicalised by out of. A fourth way in which we interact with bounded LMs is when we enter, pass from one side to another and exit, as when walking from room to room in a building. Thus, we can experience a bounded LM as a passage-way with a source location and a highlighted end-point (or goal). This relation is captured by through.

Vandeloise has been one of the most forthright advocates for the view that particles such as prepositions cannot be equated solely with spatial elements. Consider the diagram provided in Figure 6. Vandeloise observed that an image such as that depicted in Figure 6 could be construed as being either a bottle or a lightbulb. However, while we can felicitously describe the relation between the lightbulb, the TR, and its LM, the socket, as in (8):

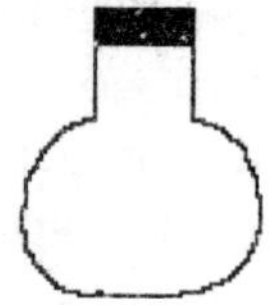

Figure 6. After Vandeloise.

(8) The bulb is in the socket

we cannot felicitously describe the relation between a bottle and its putative LM, the cap, in terms of the spatial relation designated by in:

(9) The bottle is in the cap

Vandeloise points out that as the spatial relation holding between the TR and LM in each of these sentences is identical, and yet (8) is fine while (9) is semantically anomalous, a spatial-geometric configuration alone cannot account for the relation described by in, or any other spatial particle. He argues that the relevant factor accounting for the contrast in acceptability between sentences (8) and (9) is functional: "while the socket exerts a force on the bulb and determines its position, the opposite occurs with the cap and the bottle."

Put another way, not only is the position and hence successful functioning of the bulb contingent on being in (i.e., contained by) the socket, the socket also prevents the bulb from falling to the ground and thus provides a constraining or supportive element. In contrast, the position and successful functioning of the bottle is not contingent on being in the cap.

Herskovits has also emphasised that geometric-spatial relations are not sufficient to explain the complete range of spatial uses commonly associated with spatial particles. For instance, she noted that in applies to a wide range of spatial scenes, many of which do not require that the TR is enclosed by the LM. For example, in can be employed in the sentence The pear is in the bowl to describe a spatial scene in which the bowl holds so many pieces of fruit beneath the pear, that it is physically higher than the rim of the bowl, and hence not strictly enclosed within the LM.

She argued that the fact that native speakers of English can use in to describe spatial scenes of this kind indicates that principles beyond spatial-geometric relations must be involved. The observation that the lexeme in is associated with a functional relation (in additional to purely spatial properties) has also been noted by Sinha and Jensen de López 4, as well as researchers involved in language acquisition and psycholinguistic experimentation.

We now turn to the four functional elements we will consider. We begin with the functional notion of orientation. Orientation arises as a consequence of spatio-geometric asymmetry of the TR (or LM), resulting in asymmetric perceptual access.

Orientation (with the asymmetric perceptual access and directional bias it affords) is a consequence of the morphology, in the biological sense, of animate entities. Hence, orientation is a functional consequence of physiology. In order to illustrate the notion of orientation, consider the sentence in (10):

(10) The soldier stood still facing east

In this sentence, the TR, the soldier, is functionally asymmetrical with respect to the LM. That is, the TR's inherent front-back asymmetry allows the TR to be directed to or from the LM, designated by the cardinal location east (and hence facilitates asymmetric perceptual access, canonical direction of motion, etc.). Being directed with respect to a LM is to be oriented with respect to the LM. Importantly, being oriented does not entail that the TR undergoes motion, as is evident from this example of a static TR.

We now turn to a consideration of trajectory. While motion relates to change of location, trajectory relates to the "shape" of the motion event. This represents a departure from previous analyses. Our view is that the trajectory is inseparable from a motile TR and represents the course of motion the TR undergoes. Put another way, a trajectory is a functional consequence of the particular spatial locations occupied by a particular TR as it undergoes motion.

The trajectory or "shape" of the motion is integrated into a coherent concept independent of the motion itself. This follows as we are able to conceive of TRs executing particular "shapes" even when such trajectories do not objectively exist in the world, but rather, result from integrating a series of distinct albeit contiguous locations occupied by a particular TR in memory. The following example evidences the functional element of trajectory:

(11) The stunt plane performed a perfect loop-the-loop at the air-show

In this example the expression loop-the-loop describes a particular trajectory, conceived as circular. Hence, a trajectory is a functional consequence of a TR's motion. As we argue English prepositions do not denote motion, we argue that they cannot denote a trajectory. As being oriented does not entail motion, neither does it entail a trajectory.

In view of the foregoing, we now consider how the functional notion of path is distinct from that of trajectory. Path, while related to trajectory, is a consequence of an end-point, conceived of as a goal, being related to a starting-point or locational source by virtue of a series of contiguous points. That is, the concept of path requires a particular spatial goal. In so far as a goal implicates intentionality, intention to realise the particular goal is what distinguishes a goal from just any end-point. The spatial goal is achieved by being connected to a spatial source by virtue of a series of contiguous points.

As noted, path is a functional element, which arises due to the way we interact with and reach goals, given that we act with intention and begin from a particular starting-point or locational source. Accordingly, this concept is distinct from those of trajectory and motion. In particular, as a path is conceived as relating a source with a goal, it is conceptualised as facilitating passage, which is why prototypical paths provide a particular material and conventional means of trans locating potential obstacles, e.g., tunnels, bridges, footpaths, roads, etc.. For instance, in the following sentence:

(12) The tunnel through Vale Mountain was finished in the 1980s

by virtue of a tunnel existing in (12), passage from one side of an otherwise impenetrable barrier, the mountain, is facilitated, whether or not the spatial scene involves a TR capable of undergoing motion. It is this notion of a particular relation between a source and a goal and the accompanying notion of facilitation of passage, conceptually independent of a motile TR and its trajectory, which constitutes the concept of path.

Further evidence for the functional notion of path absent motion comes from scenes involving "traces" of a TR's passage, even when the TR itself is no longer apparent. For instance, a line of trampled grass transecting a field or a smoke-trail across the sky, are labelled paths, even though the respective TRs, e.g., a person and a plane, are no longer in view. However, a means of passage, such as a tunnel, or a "trace" of passage are merely associated with the notion of path, rather than constituting the notion.

We reiterate that the concept of path concerns a starting-point or locational source being related to an endpoint conceptualised as a goal by virtue of a series of contiguous points intervening between the two extremities.

The functional notion of goal is closely related to that of path. While the endpoint of a path is in principle a spatial location (or an entity occupying the spatial location) equivalent to other points along the path, in many instances the endpoint has additional salience. This follows as the end-point often constitutes the motivation for the path in the first place.

Hence, a functional consequence of a highlighted spatial end-point is that it is particularly salient, in focus, and is typically the subject of intentional attempts to reach it. The notion of goal, then, is a functional consequence of the highlighted LM, which represents a particular location, being conceptualised as a highlighted end-point.

CASE OF TO

We have argued that the core spatial semantics of to designates a relation in which the TR is oriented with respect to a highlighted LM. This configuration often occurs in scenes involving a motile TR. Indeed, many previous analyses, based on examples such as the following, have assumed that motion or dynamism is an inherent part of the basic meaning associated with to:

(13) She walked/ran/went/drove/cycled to the store

However, a path-in the sense of a series of spatially contiguous locations mediating a starting point and an end-point which is conceived as a goal-is not inevitably associated with to, as illustrated by the following examples in which only orientation is apparent:

(14) a. He stood with his back to me. (TR is not oriented towards the LM)

b. The conservatory faces to the south so it gets sun all day long.

In the examples in (14) the TR is oriented vis-à-vis the LM. In these examples, motion of the TR is not implicated, nor is it made explicit that there is a path along which the TR could undergo locomotion. In order to account for the "static" reading in (14) and the "dynamic" reading in (13) one might posit that to has both an orientation and a movement sense. However, there are reasons to suspect that the "dynamic" reading apparent in (13) arises from context, rather than being a conventional meaning associated with to.

One of the charges which has been levelled against some semantic network theorists is that they may have vastly overestimated the number of distinct senses associated with a particular preposition. Sandra in particular has strongly argued for clearly articulated decision principles for determining what counts as a distinct sense in a polysemy network. In our model of principled polysemy, we offer two such criteria for determining whether a sense is distinct and instantiated in memory or whether it is a contextualised variant of a particular sense. Both of these criteria must hold for a usage to count as a distinct sense of a particular preposition. These criteria are detailed below:

(15) i) A usage counts as a distinct sense if it adds meaning not associated with any other sense

ii) A usage counts as a distinct sense if at least some of its instantiations cannot be derived from context

Clearly, the "dynamic" reading of (13) contains additional meaning with respect to the orientation reading in (14), and vice versa. This is the case as while orientation is an immanent aspect of motion (motion requires orientation), the reverse does not follow, orientation does not require motion—as evidenced by the examples in (14). Hence, the dynamic reading provides additional information not available in the orientation readings in (14). As such, the criterion in the first part of (15) is satisfied.

In terms of the second criterion, for the "dynamic" reading to count as a distinct sense, some instances of this reading must be context-independent, which is to say, they must be apparent absent a sentential context otherwise involving motion. However, a motion reading associated with *to* is apparent only when a verb of motion is supplied. While orientation is apparent in all the examples involving *to*, i.e., those in (13) and (14), motion is only licensed in specific contexts, namely involving verbs of motion. In this, the motion reading associated with *to* appears to be contingent upon sentential context, and hence constitutes a situated implicature of dynamism.

Despite our claim that *to* does not at base provide a dynamic meaning element, *to* can readily participate in utterances in which a dynamic reading derives. This follows as not only is *to* associated with the notion of orientation, it is additionally associated with the functional notion of goal. After all, a consequence of being oriented with respect to a particular LM which is highlighted is that in many cases the LM constitutes an objective or goal, which motivated the orientation in the first place.

There are a number of lines of evidence to support this view. For instance, consider the contrast between to and toward(s):

(16) a. He ran to the shop

b. He ran towards the shop

In (16) a the typical interpretation is that the TR is directed with respect to the LM, the shop, and that this LM constitutes the TR's goal. A consequence of the motion verb, in conjunction with to, is that a path is evoked, resulting in a reading in which the TR did indeed arrive at the shop. In contrast, in (24) b the typical reading is a TR moving in the direction of the LM, which is referenced by virtue of a convenient LM, the shop. That is, the shop is not the focused end point, but simply provides a means of referencing the general direction with respect to which the TR is oriented. One consequence of this is that even with the same verb of motion it is not entailed that the TR arrives at the shop.

Further evidence that supports the characterisation of the LM as goal comes from examples of the following kind:

(17) As Jim was being verbally attacked in the meeting, he looked to his linemanager (for support)

The verb look normally collocates with at. Yet, in this example the TR, Jim, is looking at the LM, his line-manager for a particular reason, namely for verbal support.

Accordingly, the orientation of the gaze is motivated by a particular goal, i.e., his linemanager seated at a particular location, and potential support, hence the use of to. Interestingly, in this sentence a path reading is evoked, because we conceive of sight as involving a linear "path", while there is no motion involved. A final line of evidence for the LM as goal functional element comes from examples of the following kind:

(18) He runs (past the quarry) to the hills everyday

A consequence of being oriented with respect to a particular LM, the hills, is that the LM serves as the goal or objective. For instance, (18) conveys more than that the TR is oriented (and indeed moving in the direction of) the hills, but that reaching the hills constitutes the TR's objective, as part of a fitness regimen, perhaps. Moreover, this information is more than just background knowledge, which is implicit, but actually surfaces in the semantic acceptability of prepositions. After all, the sentence in (19).

(19) #He runs to the quarry everyday [Goal: the hills]

cf. He runs past the quarry everyday [Goal: the hills]

would be semantically odd if the end-point of the run is the hills, and the quarry is only half way between the runner's home and the hills. This is so, even if the runner is oriented in the direction of the quarry. This follows as to provides information about the runner's goal, which is to reach a particular point, at a given distance from the starting point before turning around and running back. In other words, as the goal constitutes the highlighted end-point of a TR's movement, as described in §4, to cannot be employed in an utterance in which a TR is related to a point other than the highlighted LM, as illustrated by the anomaly of (19).

A proto-scene is an abstraction ultimately arising from recurring real-world spatial scenarios and represents an attempt to model the core spatial semantics (the primary or central sense) for a particular preposition. It constitutes a highly schematic TR-LM representation together with attendant functional elements which commonly result from such a configuration.

In the proto-scene for to, to denotes a spatial relation in which an oriented TR is directed toward a highlighted LM. Within this spatial configuration, the highlighted status of the LM makes it readily interpretable as a primary goal. Hence, the functional element associated with to is the LM as goal. Figure 7 represents the proto-scene for to. The black circle represents the TR. The arrow represents the orientation.

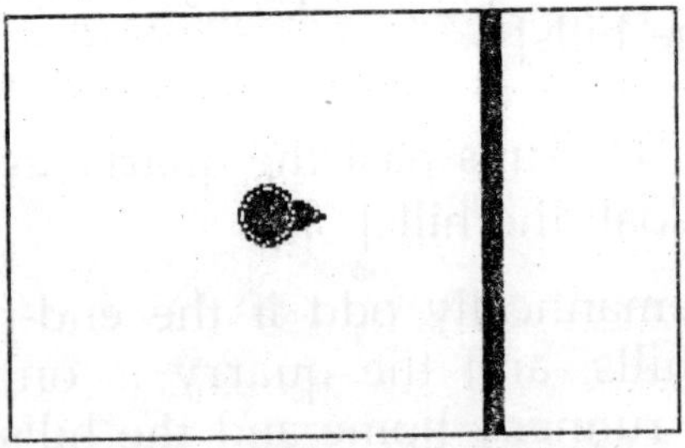

Figure 7. The proto-scene for to

The vertical line represents the LM. Note that the LM is in bold, indicating that the LM is profiled. The functional element associated with the proto-scene is that the LM constitutes the TR's goal.

In sum, what the foregoing discussion reveals is that whether either path or motion is evoked depends upon sentential context and how the semantics of the preposition (and the other elements) interact. Hence, the interpretation that the TR reaches the LM in (16)a is a consequence of interaction of a particular set of sentential elements, while in (17) there is no sense of motion, and while a path is evoked, the TR is not understood as physically "arriving at" the LM's location.

In this way, the present perspective posits that the interaction of the set of elements in question gives rise to "distributed" meaning, while also retaining the position that individual lexical items do have conventional meaning elements or senses associated with them.

Moreover, this does not necessitate the claim that to must be contributing a path meaning element. As the functional element associated with to is that of the LM as goal, a consequence of this is that when integrated with a motion verb, the TR's orientation, together with the functional element of goal gives rise to the evocation of a path, as in (17), or a reading of motion as in (16)a. It is these contextualised readings of "movement" which some scholars have attributed to the preposition to.

CASE OF THROUGH

We now turn to a consideration of through. While the spatial relation designated by through relates to the structural elements interior, boundary and exterior, and hence a bounded LM, it comprises additional structural elements which we term entrance-point, exit-point, and the contiguous locations between the entrance-point and exit-point.

In other words, the proto-scene for through designates a spatial relation in which the TR is held to occupy a contiguous series of spatial points, with respect to a LM, which has an interior structural element, such that these points are located on the exterior side of the LM coincident with the entrance point, within the LM, and on the exterior side of the LM opposite to the entrance point, i.e., the exit point.

The entrance point is understood as the locational source and the exit point as the goal. A consequence of the particular spatial designation associated with through is that the functional notion of path is evoked.

Path is a functional element, which arises due to the way we interact with and reach goals (the exit-point associated with through), given that we begin from a particular starting-point or locational source (the entrance-point associated with through). Accordingly, this concept is distinct from those of trajectory, goal, orientation and motion. For instance, in the following sentence:

(20) The tunnel through Vale Mountain was finished in the 1980s

by virtue of a tunnel existing in (20), passage from one side of an otherwise impenetrable barrier, the mountain, is facilitated, whether or not the scene involves a TR capable of undergoing motion.

As through characterises a spatial relation denoting a TR and a bounded LM in which two locations on either side of a LM are related (the entrance-point and exit-point respectively), the associated functional element is that of path. As such, the path is held to be conceptually distinct from the motion often associated with it.

Interestingly, as paths are often associated with motion,[9] motion can be evoked due to background knowledge, even in spatial scenes, which are wholly non-dynamic in nature, as in (21) below:

(21) a. The sunlight shone through the glass door

b. I sensed the cold through the glass door

In the example in (21) a, there is no (perceptible) motion associated with the spatial scene, Indeed, motion is typically coded by verbs, which involve events evolving through time. As through is a preposition and hence atemporal it does not code for motion. However, by virtue of through being employed, the notion of a path is salient, which strongly correlates with the idea of the TR physically passing or having passed from one side of the TR to the other. For instance, the sunlight is conceived as physically having passed from one side of the door to the other in (21) a.

In (21) b the cold is sensed (and thus experienced) on one side of the door, even though it originated on the other. The use of through is strongly suggestive that the coldness is experienced by virtue of a physical transfer from one side of the door to the other.

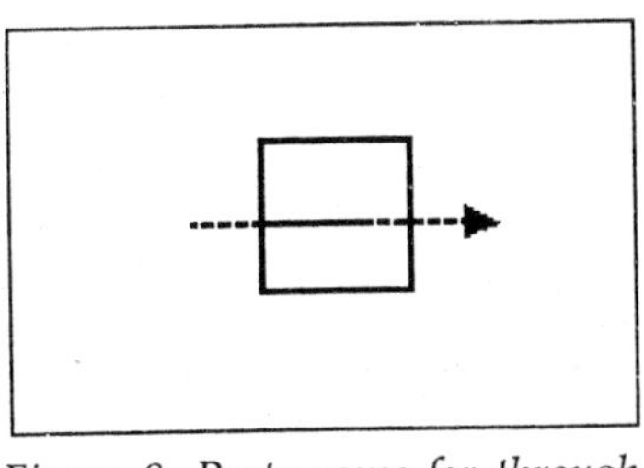

Figure 8. Proto-scene for through

Thus, the relation described by through describes a spatial relation in which a bounded LM is transacted by virtue of an entrance point and an exit point. The functional element evoked is that of path. For this reason through is often associated with motion. The proto-scene for through is diagrammed in Figure 8.

9

Grammatical Analysis of Prepositions

In the majority of works on prepositions spatial aspect of their meanings is considered to be the most representative. For example, Dirven begins with characterising 'spatial conceptualisations' of twelve prepositions and sets of various relationships that obtain among them. Next, he establishes 'chains of meaning from physical into mental space', from spatial domains via the domain of time to the more abstract ones such as: state, topic or area, manner/means, circumstance and cause/reason.

Concluding, Dirven points to 'the relationship between the way physical space is divided up in English and the way mental space is structured'. In other words, the author's position is that the 'basis of it all is the conceptualisation of physical space'.

Dirven's position can be regarded as typical of cognitive analyses of prepositions in that it follows the pattern in which the first step is to characterise the type of organisation in three-dimensional space the preposition in focus encodes, and then proceed to metaphorical extensions of the structures into abstract domains. Length in Turewicz is that the spatial basis of prepositions is crucial to the evolution leading to the formation of meaning schemata of prepositions (indeed, each of the predicates), whereas 'speciality' need not retain the central position in the meaning structure of the schema which sanctions specific meanings (of a preposition).

COGNITIVE GRAMMAR ANALYSIS

In Cognitive Grammar all language structure is symbolic in that "morphological and syntactic structures themselves are inherently symbolic, above and beyond the symbolic relations embodied in the lexical items they employ". This means that grammatical categories (noun, verb, preposition, etc.), grammatical morphemes (the, -ed, -s, etc.) and grammatical rules (e.g. plural formation) are characterisable as conceptual structures on a par with lexical items.

More precisely, from the perspective of linguistic analysis, a relevant difference between conceptual content of grammatical categories (e.g. prepositions) and content words reduces to a higher level of schematicity involved in the characterisation of semantic structures of the former.

In still other words, the conceptual content may be highly schematic but, nevertheless, is definable by means of analytic tools applicable for the characterisation of lexical items. The profile / base alignment is at the heart of semantic analysis of all language structure.

Profile / Base Alignment

For Langacker the relation of symbolisation consists in the reciprocal symbolic relationship between a semantic value—the semantic pole of a symbolic structure—and its phonological representation—the phonological pole. To say that all language structure is symbolic means that a full characterisation of a language expression involves defining the values of its semantic and phonological poles.

A linguistic explication of the semantic pole of a symbolic structure—the predication—requires reference to respective 'portions' of the knowledge system we acquire and reorganise throughout our lives. In Cognitive Grammar framework the 'portions' of knowledge system are referred to as cognitive domains. In brief, cognitive domains are concepts which provide cognitive contexts for the characterisation of semantic poles of language structures. Typically, an exhaustive characterisation of a predication—semantic structure—requires reference to a matrix of domains. Let us take the predicate [TREE] as an example.

In view of the above, a semantic structure derives its linguistic value from certain substructures of the knowledge system organised into matrices of cognitive domains. Hence, a characterisation of the semantic value [TREE] requires

(i) identification of the domains indispensable for the formation of the concept tree—a mental category;

(ii) specifying substructures (in the domains) directly relevant for the concept specification;

(iii) discovering the organisation of the conceptual content as a constitutive factor of meaning structure—a linguistic category.

Following the procedure defined in (i)—(iii), as the first step towards a Cognitive Grammar characterisation of [TREE] an analyst will identify the fragments of our knowledge system which condition, first, the possibility of concept formation and, consequently, categorisation of a fragment of reality in terms of the concept.

Allowing a slightly naïve argumentation, the process of discovering and defining the semantic structure of a predicate can be characterised as follows. To identify the domains an analyst can ask a question of the type: What kind of knowledge is indispensable for learning what a tree is and recognising some elements of the surrounding reality as trees?. An answer can be the following: to understand what the tree is and how it differs from non—trees, one has to mentally refer to three-dimensional space (3-DS) (a picture with a tree is not a real tree) and its substructure representing shapes; the domain of colour (DC); the representation (domain) of touch sensations (DT); the representation of basic division of the entities of the world into animate and non-animate, the domain of natural entities and artefacts (DBDNA).

From the matrix of domains, in accordance with (ii), the analyst derives the substructures directly relevant for the categorisation judgment (as a cognitive act) and thus relevant for semantic specification (a linguistic act): a tall object of characteristic shape broadening in the upper part and cylinder—like base (3DS); the upper—broader part of green colour, the cylinder—like base of dark brown, grey, black (DC); the surface of the green elements soft, the surface of the trunk rough and hard (DT); subject to the changes in nature—undergoes the phases characteristic of natural entities of the world: growth, maturity and death (DBDNA).

Finally, as specified in (iii) (discovering the organisation of the conceptual content as a constitutive factor of meaning structure—a linguistic category), an adequate characterisation of the predicate [TREE] requires discovering and defining the way the specifications discerned above are organised.

Precisely, for a categorising individual to identify an object as a tree she / he has to simultaneously evoke all relevant substructures in the matrix of domains: shape itself cannot differentiate between a tree and a tower; colour itself cannot differentiate between a tree and a painted building, etc.

All in all, it seems legitimate to assume that the process of concept formation involves the process of organising relevant content of relevant domains in such a way that interconnections of special type obtain among the specifications.

Namely, conceptualising the knowledge system as a vast network of concepts related through numerous nods (each of the nods being itself a concept), it is possible to view the structure of concept as a network formed of substructures relevant for the formation of the concept 'meeting' at one nod. In other words, a concept formation requires content specifications to be organised around a nod related to all of them, as a cognitive (and hence semantic) value of the concept is determined by the alignment between the shared nod and the specifications.

Langacker postulated the notion of profile/base alignment to grasp and characterise semantic values corresponding to respective parts of knowledge system organised as local networks. The base of the alignment is formed of the specifications in relevant domains, whereas the profile is the nod shared by all specification relations.

Langacker formalises this relationship introducing the notion of scope to be understood as 'the array of conceptual content it evokes', whereas the profiled structure in the base is the designatum of the predication.

In still other words, for each of the networks the shared nod attains special status of designatum and defines the profile of the semantic pole, whereas the specification relations the nod participates in—the scope of predication—form its base. Profile and base constitute inseparable facets to the definition of the semantic pole; neither of them itself can characterise the value of a predication. Indeed, it is the alignment between the two that defines the semantic pole of a symbolic structure.

Schematicity and Prototype

Discussing the procedures involved in concept

formation and deriving semantic structure in the form of profile / base alignment. Although fairly specific, the category can be simultaneously viewed as fairly schematic.

Namely, on the one hand, the language expression can operate in all categorising judgments, when a speakers faces the fragment of reality that 'agrees' with the profile/base alignment defining the meaning of the word, i.e. conceptual content of the lexical category.

On the other hand, the profile/base alignment defining the semantic structure of the lexical category tree is highly abstract, too abstract to differentiate among various kinds of tree. Cognitive Grammar formally accommodates this aspect of categorisation in terms of schematicity relation within a category.

In brief, on the basis of specifications characterising members of a category, there develops a superordinate structure, the schema, which is compatible with the meaning structures of its instantiations, i.e. specific category members.

Within a category structure every higher level entity functions as a schema for a lower level entity; the relationship consists in that the schema lacks in specifications of finer details of its instantiations. For example, the predicate tree is less specific than oak tree or apple tree Finally, the schematicity relation can be full if the schema and its instantiations are fully compatible in their specifications; it is partial if the specifications are only partially compatible.

The schematicity relation pertains to all language structure. Precisely by the same process of schematisation, regularities observable in sets of complex language expressions allow for the extraction of constructional schemes which describe types of grammatical constructions, i.e. grammatical rules. Langacker defines them as "templates reflecting in abstract terms the symbolic compositionality observable across arrays of complex expressions".

Along with the categorisation by the schema, Langacker acknowledges the role of prototype for the category structure. Namely, where schematisation pertains to the vertical dimension of the category, the horizontal dimension within the structure of the category incorporates the process of extension (including metaphorical extensions).

Here the category membership is defined by the degree of closeness of a given member to the prototype. The prototype 'initiates' chains of extensions on the basis of perceived similarity of two category members, one of which functions as more prototypical category member for the other.

Langacker views the two types of processes involved in the category formation as closely related:

> In the formation of a complex category, consequently, outward growth from the prototype tends to co-occur with upward growth.

In other words, to the extent an extension from a prototype involves grasping some similarity between two category members, the similarity allows for the extraction of some schema which sanctions category membership of both.

Symbolic Nature of the Category Preposition

Langacker argues for the characterisation of grammatical categories by means of schemas, which reflect the commonality of all category members. To reflect the commonality within a category, its schema must be necessarily highly abstract in both its semantic and phonological poles.

Nonetheless, despite the high degree of schematicity, the type of categorisation is revealing to the extent it provides the foundation for distinguishing one grammatical class from the others. With respect to traditional grammatical categories, Cognitive Grammar differentiates between two types of symbolic structure.

The symbolic structure whose semantic pole profiles a conceptual region characterises the content of the grammatical category noun, whereas the conceptual content of other grammatical categories, i.e. verbs, prepositions, adverbs, etc., has the profile of relation.

Nouns as conceptual regions

The semantic structure of the grammatical category noun is characterised, like any other semantic structure, as a predication whose value derives from the alignment between a certain structure—the profile—and the portion in the matrix of cognitive domains which constitutes direct conceptual context of the structure—its base.

Langacker states that 'every nominal predication designates a region'. This special type of profile means that the content of the base is accessible through the profile as a homogenous whole, a region whose extension is determined by the conceptual richness incorporated in the specification relations.

Accordingly, the conceptual region profiled by [OAK TREE] incorporates more specifications in its base than that profiled by [TREE], hence the two predicates differ in that the profiled regions differ with respect to degree of specification of (conceptual) content (and bounding).

Formally, the internal structure of the conceptual region is characterised as a 'set of interconnected entities'. Importantly, despite the fact that the internal structure of a region can be both fairly complex and dynamic, the interconnections

> are not themselves profiled by a nominal predication; they serve to establish a set of entities as a region, but are not per se constitutive of the region. (...) the profiling of the interconnected entities is collective: the region as a whole (...) functions as a designatum and constitutes one instance of the [THING] category.

In other words, the profile of a region abstracts away from details of individual entities and 'ignores' the possible diversity within the profiled region, foregrounding its conceptual homogeneity. Just like homogeneity of a region is a mental process, so is the bounding of the region, defined by Langacker as 'some limit to the set of interconnected entities it comprises'.

Hence, bounding is not to be understood in linear terms. For example, [TREE] profiles a region whose internal structure can be described as a set of specifications: shape specification, colour sensations, touch sensation, and taxonomy qualification, organised in a specific way.

Both content and its organisation define conceptual boundaries of the predicate. Any departure from the specific profile/base alignment means 'changing the boundaries' of the concept, thus formation of another concept.

The schema of the grammatical category noun is represented as a symbolic unit of the form: [THING / x]. In the formula, [THING] indicates the semantic pole of the symbolic unit, whereas its phonological pole is indicated by [x] to signal a broad array of possible phonetic realisations.

Relations

A conceptual region is formed of a set of interconnected entities, however, their relational character is downgraded because the interconnections in the nominal profile are conceptualised holistically. It should be borne in mind that each of the interconnections individually is a relation whose individuality is suppressed by a collective conceptualisation within a higher-order cognitive entity—region.

The conceptualisation in which rather than a region within a certain cognitive structure, a relation between two entities of this structure is designated derives an alternative to the nominal profile, i.e. the relational profile. The difference between the grammatical category noun and other grammatical categories resides in the nature of the profile. Namely, where in the case of nouns a set of relations will be profiled as a whole, for other grammatical categories one relation between chosen substructures—an interconnection—may be 'chosen' as the designatum.

Crucial to the characterisation of relational profile is the fact that in this type of profile/base alignment three elements are foregrounded simultaneously: the relation and the entities participating in the relation.

In other words, predications with the relational profile are conceptually dependent, because any instance of conceptualising a relation between two entities involves conceptualising the participants. As Langacker puts it "one cannot conceptualise interconnections without also conceptualising the entities that they interconnect".

The dependence of relational predications can be a factor distinguishing between nouns and other grammatical categories on the level grammatical integration.

Precisely, because in the profile of a region no salient internal reference is made to any structure from the outside of the region, the nominal profile is conceptually autonomous. As regards the internal structure of relations, one of the participants can be autonomous and the other dependent. Thus, with respect to conceptual dependence, there may be a noticeable asymmetry between entities within the relational profile.

Trajector /landmark asymmetry

The asymmetry pertaining to the internal structure of relational predications is connected with salience of its participants.

The status of the participants is not equal as one of them is a figure in the relational predication (is to be elaborated by the figure of the conceptualisation), whereas other salient participants, often referred to as secondary figures, are called by Langacker landmarks. The very term 'landmark' is motivated by the fact that "they are naturally viewed (in prototypical instances) as providing points of reference for locating the trajector".

Viewed from the perspective of potential integration of relational entities with other entities on a higher level of cognitive organisation, i.e. the process of meaning formation of complex language expressions, the trajector and landmark(s) may function as elaboration sites (e-sites).

Langacker introduces the term to refer to the substructure in the structure of a relational entity which schematically defines the predication with which the entity can integrate. In other words, e-site is the substructure in the semantic structure of relation which bears the schematicity relation with respect to the language expression which can integrate with the relation; the e-site functions as a schema for the language expression to integrate with the relational predication.

So defined relational profile constitutes the foundation for characterising the conceptual structure of grammatical categories other than noun.

The differentiation within the relational schema into verbs, on the one hand, and adjectives, adverbs, prepositions, affixes, etc., on the other one, derives from specifications of the schemas for each of the relational categories: verbs categorise as temporal relations as the temporal domain figures in their profile.

The other relational subcategories are referred to as atemporal relations. The set of atemporal relations can be further differentiated on the basis of specifications of the elaboration sites defining schematically the profiles of the entities participating in the relations—trajector and landmark(s).

COGNITIVE GRAMMAR ANALYSIS OF [IN]

Relational Profile of the Preposition

One of fundamental theses in CG conception of language structure is that semantic structure of any degree of complexity is characterisable in terms of one profile/base alignment.

Consequently, if two predications integrate, the result of the integration is not a sum of their meanings but a new composite (semantic) structure encoded in a 'new' profile/base alignment. What follows from this formulation is that the meaning of a preposition 'by itself', e.g. in is encoded by a profile/base alignment different from the profile/base alignment defining the meaning of a prepositional phrase, where the preposition is followed by a specific noun, e.g. in a cup.

Specifically, in the process of prepositional phrase formation (a composite semantic structure with a relational predicate and elaborated landmark), the semantic structure of the prepositional object (the noun phrase following the preposition) contributes to the profile/base alignment of the composite structure.

The meaning integration of two semantic structures is possible due to correspondences between them specified schematically by respective elaboration-sites (e-sites). In the case of prepositions, the elaboration site (e-site) of the landmark schematically characterises the nominal entities to elaborate the landmark (the prepositional objects / complements).

To the extent the e-site bears the relation of schematicity to these nominals, it restricts the list of predicates capable of elaborating the landmark (instantiations) to the nouns whose specifications are at least partly compatible with the specifications profiled by the landmark esite.

Putting the above in other words, on the first level of integration (when the prepositional phrase is formed) the elaboration of the landmark specifies the relation profiled by in as in the landmark. Accordingly, the trajector e-site (the schematic profile of the trajector entity) is determined by the relation in the landmark rather than in.

The characterisation may be schematic but it provides foundation for the explanations of more specific cases. To the extent specifications of the landmark specify the conceptual content of the prepositional phrase, the more specific meaning of the phrase restricts the array of entities capable of elaborating its trajector.

In brief, the meaning structure of the nominal entity that follows the preposition, having integrated with the type of prepositional schema, specifies the type of in-relation thus restricting the array of the nominals capable of entering the 'in the landmark' relation.

For example, in the milk in the cup, the specifications of cup derive the prepositional phrase in the cup. As a symbolic (composite) structure, the phrase is characterisable by profile/base alignment in which the profile remains relational but the base incorporates specifications of the cup.

As a result, because the schematic composite structure in the landmark changes into more specific one in the cup, a new semantic structure is formed whose trajector e-site will be accordingly specified.

Simply, while in the prepositional phrase in the landmark the trajector e-site allows unconstrained choice of nominal and relational elaborations, specifications of the landmark in the cup restrict the choice of the trajector to entities capable of interacting with the relation in the cup, though irrespective of whether a nominal the milk or a process, as in the genii are cleaning up in the cup, elaborate the trajector.

Needless to say, the specifications of the e-site of the prepositional phrase in the cup exclude, despite its schematicity, such elaborations of the trajector as ?the girl and boy are cleaning up in the cup, unless the nominal the cup departs from its prototypical meaning, or the expression structures a scene from a mental space of fiction.

There is one more facet to the meaning integration of the trajector and landmark of in, which is directly related to the qualities of the scene under conceptualisation structured by respective language expressions. Consider the scene described by milk in the cup. Two real world entities are organised in a specific way because their qualities allow the organisation.

The qualities involved are the 'shape and solid surface' of cup and the quality 'liquid' of milk. Surprising as the observation may appear, the organisation of elements is determined by the compatibility of respective qualities rather than the fact that one of the objects has all characteristics of a cup, whereas the other has all characteristics of milk.

In other words, the qualities: 'shape, solid surface' and 'liquid' are the elements in the structures of the objects which define the way they can interact. In linguistic terms, the qualities of the objects are encoded in the base of respective profile/ base alignments.

The fact that these specifications represent the qualities allowing the type of organisation encoded in milk in the cup is grasped in Cognitive Grammar framework by the concept of active zone.

Precisely, an active zone of a predication is the substructure in the structure of the predication directly interacting with the structure of the other predication in the process of meaning integration. The notion of active zone differs from the elaboration site in terms of schematicity. While the e-site schematically characterises the profile of the predicate to elaborate either the landmark or trajector, the notion of active zone refers to specific substructures in the predications elaborating the landmark and the trajector.

Employing Langacker's notational system, the result of the process of integration deriving a prepositional phrase can be represented as follows:

[PREP/z] -- [THING/x] [PREP--THING]/[z --x],

(where 'z' and 'x' stand for the phonological poles). This constructional schema sanctions the more specific one in which the preposition is specified by the predicate [IN/in].

Crucial to the analysis postulated above is the fact that once the schema [PREP/z] is specified as [IN/in], the other element in the constructional schema also gets specified to sanction only these nominals which are schematically characterised by the landmark e-site of [IN], which can be represented as [$_{IN}$THING/y]. In this fashion the constructional schema for the prepositional phrase headed by the preposition in will be represented by the following formula:

[IN/in] -- [$_{IN}$THING/y] [IN-- $_{IN}$THING] / [in -- y]

By virtue of its relational profile, the predication [IN--$_{IN}$THING] schematically defines its higher level valence relations in the structure of the trajector e-site. As reflected by the notation, because the semantic structure of the relational predicate [IN] is more schematic than the semantic structure of [IN--

$_{\text{IN}}$THING], the trajector e-site of the former will differ in schematicity from the latter.

Precisely by the same principle, once the [$_{\text{IN}}$THING/y] is elaborated by a specific nominal, e.g. [$_{\text{IN}}$THING1/y1], the more specific symbolic structure [IN -- $_{\text{IN}}$THING$_1$] / [in -- y_1] will incorporate the more specific trajector e-site, thus narrowing the range of entities with which the predication can integrate.

10

Detection of Prepositional Errors

The National Clearinghouse for English Language Acquisition estimates that 9.6% of the students in the US public school population speak a language other than English and have limited English proficiency. Clearly, there is a substantial and increasing need for tools for instruction in English as a Second Language (ESL). In particular, preposition usage is one of the most difficult aspects of English grammar for non-native speakers to master.

Preposition errors account for a significant proportion of all ESL grammar errors. They represented the largest category, about 29%, of all the errors by 53 intermediate to advanced ESL students, and 18% of all errors reported in an intensive analysis of one Japanese writer. Preposition errors are not only prominent among error types, they are also quite frequent in ESL writing.

Dalgish analysed the essays of 350 ESL college students representing 15 different native languages and reported that preposition errors were present in 18% of sentences in a sample of text produced by writers from first languages as diverse as Korean,

Greek, and Spanish. The goal of the research described here is to provide software for detecting common grammar and usage errors in the English writing of non-native English speakers. Our work targets errors involving prepositions, specifically those of incorrect preposition selection, such as arrive to the town, and those of extraneous prepositions, as in most of people.

ISSUES OF PREPOSITION USAGE

Why are prepositions so difficult to master? Perhaps it is because they perform so many complex roles. In English, prepositions appear in adjuncts, they mark the arguments of predicates, and they combine with other parts of speech to express new meanings. The choice of preposition in an adjunct is largely constrained by its object (in the summer, on Friday, at noon) and the intended meaning (at the beach, on the beach, near the beach, by the beach). Since adjuncts are optional and tend to be flexible in their position in a sentence, the task facing the learner is quite complex.

Prepositions are also used to mark the arguments of a predicate. Usually, the predicate is expressed by a verb, but sometimes it takes the form of an adjective (He was fond of beer), a noun (They have a thirst for knowledge), or a nominalisation (The child's removal from the classroom). The choice of the preposition as an argument marker depends on the type of argument it marks, the word that fills the argument role, the particular word used as the predicate, and whether the predicate is a nominalisation. Even with these constraints, there are still variations in the ways in which arguments can be expressed. Levin catalogues verb alternations such as They loaded hay on the wagon vs. They loaded the wagon with hay, which show that, depending on the verb, an argument may sometimes be marked by a preposition and sometimes not.

English has hundreds of phrasal verbs, consisting of a verb and a particle (some of which are also prepositions). To complicate matters, phrasal verbs are often used with prepositions (i.e., give up on someone; give in to their demands). Phrasal verbs are particularly difficult for non-native speakers to master because of their non-compositionality of meaning, which forces the learner to commit them to rote memory.

RELATED WORK

If mastering English prepositions is a daunting task for the second language learner, it is even more so for a computer. To our knowledge, only three other groups have attempted to automatically detect errors in preposition usage. Eeg-Olofsson et al. used 31 handcrafted matching rules to detect extraneous, omitted, and incorrect prepositions in Swedish text written by native speakers of English, Arabic, and Japanese. The rules, which were based on the kinds of errors that were found in a training set of text produced by non-native Swedish writers, targeted spelling errors involving prepositions and some particularly problematic Swedish verbs. In a test of the system, 11 of 40 preposition errors were correctly detected.

Izumi et al. and used errorannotated transcripts of Japanese speakers in an interview-based test of spoken English to train a maximum entropy classifier to recognise 13 different types of grammatical and lexical errors, including errors involving prepositions.

The classifier relied on lexical and syntactic features. Overall performance for the 13 error types reached 25.1% precision with 7.1% recall on an independent test set of sentences from the same source, but the researchers do not separately report the results for preposition error detection. The approach taken by Izumi and colleagues is most similar to the one we have used.

More recently, used a language model and stochastic grammar to replace prepositions removed from a dialogue corpus. Even though they reported a precision of 0.88 and recall of 0.78, their evaluation was on a very restricted domain with only a limited number of prepositions, nouns and verbs.

SELECTION MODEL

A preposition error can be a case of incorrect preposition selection (They arrived to the town), use of a preposition in a context where it is prohibited (They came to inside), or failure to use a preposition in a context where it is obligatory (e.g., He is fond this book). To detect the first type of error, incorrect selection, we have employed a maximum entropy (ME) model to estimate the probability of each of 34 prepositions, based on the features in their local contexts.

The ME Principle says that the best model will satisfy the constraints found in the training, and for those situations not covered in the training, the best model will assume a distribution of maximum entropy. This approach has been shown to perform well in combining heterogeneous forms of evidence, as in word sense disambiguation. It also has the desirable property of handling interactions among features without having to rely on the assumption of feature independence, as in a Naive Bayesian model.

Our ME model was trained on 7 million "events" consisting of an outcome (the preposition that appeared in the training text) and its associated con-text (the set of feature-value pairs that accompanied it). These 7 million prepositions and their contexts were extracted from the MetaMetrics corpus of 1100 and 1200 Lexile text (11th and 12th grade) and newspaper text from the San Jose Mercury News. The sentences were then POS-tagged and then chunked into noun phrases and verb phrases by a heuristic chunker.

The maximum entropy model was trained with 25 contextual features. Some of the features represented the words and tags found at specific locations adjacent to the preposition; others represented the head words and tags of phrases that preceded or followed the preposition. Table 1 shows a subset of the feature list.

Some features had only a few values while others had many. PHR pre is the "preceding phrase" feature that indicates whether the preposition was preceded by a noun phrase (NP) or a verb phrase

(VP). In the example in Table 2, the preposition into is preceded by an NP. In a sentence that begins After the crowd was whipped up into a frenzy of anticipation, the preposition into is preceded by a VP. There were only two feature value pairs for this feature: PHR pre NP and PHR pre VP.

Other features had hundreds or even thousands of different values because they represented the occurrence of specific words that preceded or followed a preposition. Any feature#value pairs which occurred with very low frequency in the training (less than 10 times in the 7 million contexts) were eliminated to avoid the need for smoothing their probabilities. Lemma forms of words were used as feature values to further reduce the total number and to allow the model to generalise across inflectional variants. Even after incorporating these reductions, the number of values was still very large.

ANALYSIS ON GRAMMATICAL TEXT

The model was tested on 18,157 preposition contexts extracted from 12 files randomly selected from a portion of 1100 Lexile text (11th grade) that had not been used for training. For each context, the model predicted the probability of each preposition given the contextual representation. The highest probability preposition was then compared to the preposition that had actually been used by the writer. Because the test corpus consisted of published, edited text, we assumed that this material contained few, if any, errors. In this and subsequent tests, the model was used to classify each context as one of 34 classes (prepositions).

Results of the comparison between the classifier and the test set showed that the overall proportion of agreement between the text and the classifier was 0.69. The value of kappa was 0.64. When we examined the errors, we discovered that, frequently, the classifier's most probable preposition (the one it assigned) differed from the second most probable by just a few percentage points. This corresponded to a situation in which two or more prepositions were likely to be found in a given context.

Consider the context They thanked him for his consideration this matter, where either of or in could fill the blank. Because the classifier was forced to make a choice in this and other close cases, it incurred a high probability of making an error. To avoid this situation, we re-ran the test allowing the classifier to skip any preposition if its top ranked and second ranked choices differed by less than a specified amount.

In other words, we permitted it to respond only when it was confident of its decision. When the difference between the first and second ranked choices was 0.60 or greater, 50% of the cases received no decision, but for the remaining half of the test cases, the proportion of agreement was 0.90 and kappa was 0.88. This suggests that a considerable improvement in performance can be achieved by using a more conservative approach based on a higher confidence level for the classifier.

ANALYSIS ON ESL ESSAYS

To evaluate the ME model's suitability for analysing ungrammatical text, 2,000 preposition contexts were extracted from randomly selected essays written on ESL tests by native speakers of Chinese, Japanese, and Russian. This set of materials was used to look for problems that were likely to arise as a consequence of the mismatch between the training corpus (edited, grammatical text) and the testing corpus (ESL essays with errors of various kinds). When the model was used to classify prepositions in the ESL essays, it became obvious, almost immediately, that a number of new performance issues would have to be addressed.

Table 1: Some features used in ME Model

Feature	Description	No.of values with freq ≥ 10
BGL	Bigram to left; includes preceding word and POS	23,620
BGR	Bigram to right; includes following word and POS	20,495
FH	Headword of the following phrase	19,718
FP	Following phrase	40,778
PHR pre	Preceding phrase type	2
PN	Preceding noun	18,329
PNMod	Adjective modifying preceding noun	3,267
PNP	Preceding noun phrase	29,334
PPrep	Preceding preposition	60
PV	Preceding verb	5,221
PVP	Preceding verb phrase	23,436
PVtag	POS tag of the preceding verb	24
PVword	Lemma of the preceding verb	5,221
PW	Lemma of the preceding word	2,437
TGL	Trigram to left; includes two preceding words and POS	44,446
TGR	Trigram to right; includes two following words and POS	54,906

The student essays contained many misspelled words. Because misspellings were not in the training, the model was unable to use the features associated with them in its decision making. The tagger was also affected by spelling errors, so to avoid these problems, the classifier was allowed to skip any context that contained misspelled words in positions adjacent to the preposition or in its adjacent phrasal heads.

A second problem resulted from punctuation errors in the student writing. This usually took the form of missing commas. In the training corpus, commas generally separated parenthetical expressions, such as from my point of view, from the rest of the sentence.

Without the comma, the model selected of as the most probable preposition following because, instead of from. A set of heuristics was used to locate locate common sites of comma errors and skip these contexts.

There were two other common sources of classification error: antonyms and benefactives. The model very often confused prepositions with opposite meanings (like with/without and from/to), so when the highest probability preposition was an antonym of the one produced by the writer, we blocked the classifier from marking the usage as an error.

Benefactive phrases of the form for + person/ organisation (for everyone, for my school) were also difficult for the model to learn, most likely because, as adjuncts, they are free to appear in many different places in a sentence and the preposition is not constrained by its object, resulting in their frequency being divided among many different contexts.

When a benefactive appeared in an argument position, the model's most probable preposition was generally not the preposition for. In the sentence They described a part for a kid, the preposition of has a higher probability. The classifier was prevented from marking for + person/organisation as a usage error in such contexts.

Table 2: Classifier vs. Rater Statistics

	Rater 1 vs. Rater 2	Classifier vs. Rater 1	Classifier vs. Rater 2
Agreement	0.926	0.942	0.934
Kappa	0.599	0.365	0.291
Precision	N/A	0.778	0.677
Recall	N/A	0.259	0.205

To summarise, the classifier consisted of the ME model plus a programme that blocked its application in cases of misspelling, likely punctuation errors, antonyms prepositions, and benefactives. Another difference between the training corpus and the testing corpus was that the latter contained grammatical errors.

In the sentence, This was my first experience about choose friends, there is a verb error immediately following the preposition. Arguably, the preposition is also wrong since the sequence about choose is ill-formed. When the classifier marked the preposition as incorrect in an ungrammatical context, it was credited with correctly detecting a preposition error.

Even though these filters cover just one quarter of the 142 extraneous errors, they did improve precision from 0.778 to 0.796, and recall from 0.259 to 0.304.

Bibliography

Bennett, David C., *Spatial and Temporal Uses of English Prepositions: An Essay in Stratificational Semantics*, London: Longman,. 1975.

Bitchener, S. Young, and D. Cameron, "The effect of different types of corrective feedback on esl student writing", *Journal of Second Language Writing*,. 2005.

Dalgish, G., "Computer-assisted esl research and courseware development", *Computers and Composition*, 1985.

Dirven, R., "Dividing up physical and mental space into conceptual categories by means of English prepositions", In *Zelinski-Wibelt*, C., (ed.), 1993.

Eeg-Olofsson and O. Knuttson, "Automatic grammar checking for second language learners - the use of prepositions", In *Nodalida*, 2003.

Emonds, Joseph E., *A Unified Theory of Syntactic Categories*, Dordrecht: Foris, 1985.

Haspelmath, Martin, "Adpositions", *International Encyclopedia of Linguistics*. 2nd ed. New York: Oxford University Press, 2003.

Herskovits, A., *The linguistic expression of spatial knowledge*, Duisburg: Linguistic Agency of the University of Duisburg, 1989.

Huddleston, Rodney, and Geoffrey K. Pullum, *The Cambridge Grammar of the English Language*, Cambridge: Cambridge University Press, 2002.

Izumi, K. Uchimoto, and H. Isahara, "The overview of the sst speech corpus of japanese learner english and evaluation